Putting God In His Place

Exalting God in the iCulture

By Matt Whitman, Matt Ostercamp, Aron Utecht,
and Mark Coddington

NextStep Resources
Minneapolis, MN

To our parents, who taught us to love learning
and to follow Christ.

Putting God In His Place

Distributed by:
NextStep Resources
7890 12th Ave South
Minneapolis, MN 55425
www.nsresources.com
800-444-2665

ISBN 0-911802-44-4

Table of Contents

Introduction. 9

Part I

The Church and Cultural Assumptions in
Third-Millennium America. 17

1 The Marketplace *By Matt Whitman* 19
2 Democracy and Individualism *By Aron Utecht* 35
3 Technology *By Matt Ostercamp* 49
4 Entertainment *By Mark Coddington*. 79

Part II

Introduction - Moving Forward 79
5 Let the Gospel Speak *By Aron Utecht*. 83
6 Interpret Actively and Faithfully *By Matt Whitman* 93
7 Embrace Substance *By Mark Coddington* 105
8 Strive for Simplicity *By Matt Ostercamp* 115

Conclusion 123
Appendix The Purpose of the Church *By Aron Utecht*. 125
Bibliography 135
Citations 137

Biographies

Matt Whitman worked until 2010 as a college/young adult pastor at the Grand Island Evangelical Free Church in Grand Island, Nebraska, and a history instructor at Central Community College in the same city. He currently serves at the Evangelical Free Church in Lander, Wyoming. He holds a bachelor's degree from Trinity International University in Illinois, a master's degree from Trinity Evangelical Divinity School, and a master's degree from the University of Nebraska at Kearney.

Matt Ostercamp is a librarian at the Brandel Library at North Park University in Chicago, Illinois. He holds a bachelor's degree from Trinity International University, a master's degree from Trinity Evangelical Divinity School, and a master's degree from the University of Illinois at Urbana-Champaign.

Aron Utecht is the senior pastor at Immanuel Baptist Church in Beulah, North Dakota. He holds a bachelor's degree from the University of Nebraska-Lincoln, a Master of Divinity from Denver Seminary, and a master's degree from the University of Nebraska at Kearney.

Mark Coddington is a graduate student at the University of Texas at Austin, where he studies journalism and the Internet. He is a former reporter who has worked at newspapers in Nebraska and New

PUTTING GOD IN HIS PLACE

York. A graduate of Wheaton College in Illinois, he is active in All Saints Presbyterian Church in America in Austin.

Introduction

We are children of the church. Three of us grew up in parsonages, where we got an intimate view of the study, prayer, joy, and heartbreak that lies behind the weekly ecclesiastical routine of services, kids clubs, choir practice, and board meetings. All of us continue to be nourished by the church. We've been educated by Christian schools and regularly participate as staff or laity in our local body. Unfortunately, we can't escape a nagging sense that something's a little off — that something doesn't fit quite right. This intuition has followed us as we've left the churches of our youth and worshiped in a variety of settings.

This sense of something being amiss transcends region, worship style, socioeconomic status, and even doctrine. It's present in that old-time country church with the fading clapboard siding and a few dozen members. It's present in the hip 2,000-member suburban church with a thriving singles ministry and studio-perfect worship team. And it's present in the century-old mainline Protestant church that is struggling to maintain its role in the community.

All of us are fallen; there are as many problems in churches as there are churches. But individual issues within each local church are merely symptoms of one root problem: The exaltation of the individual has become central in the American church. This glorification of the self has served to undermine the church's greatest purpose — to glorify the God who leads and loves it. This isn't usually the result of conscious pride or willful rebellion toward God; rather, it stems from submission to the voices of our culture. This fundamentally backwards ordering of the purpose of the church happens when we bring our cultural assumptions to church with us and unwittingly apply them to our faith and practice.

It is true that we are influenced by our cultural surroundings. Even those who have never sat in on a sociology class talk about this concept regularly. We do it when we complain that today's teenagers' fixation with Facebook and texting limit their ability to interact with each other in meaningful, face-to-face ways. We do it when we fret each year about the reality of Christ's birth being lost in our culture's over-commercialization of Christmas. But how often do we take it a step further and apply those ideas to our own lives and to our churches themselves? We've all critiqued the greed and competitiveness that pervade our culture, but have we, for example, thought deeply about the impact of capitalism and its assumptions on our church's priorities?

We might be tempted to think that because of its sacred nature, because its members have been called by God to be set apart, that the church can be relatively free of culture's influence. But this is simply not the case. Since its inception, the church has always existed within a specific time and place. For instance, the early church confronted the scourge of Gnosticism by articulating the truths of Christianity in creeds that drew upon concepts of classical philosophy; the medieval church developed an elaborate hierarchy to evangelize and keep order after the fall of Rome; during the 1970s and '80s the American church responded to the Baby Boomers' disillusionment with institutions by developing seeker-sensitive ministries. At every point in history, the church has dealt with new issues, trends, and cultures as they have arisen, and our age is no different. Many of the cultural realities that influence today's church most heavily are so deeply ingrained in American society that they disappear into the background and are difficult to see as the shapers they are. But make no mistake: Everything has meaning that reaches far deeper than its initial appearance. The church must be aware of these underlying ideas and engage them if it is to keep God at the center. That is why we have written this book. Even though Christians continually and rightly affirm their desire to glorify God, the cultural values we actually express in church assert just the opposite through their elevation of ourselves. We believe it is critical for the health of the church to identify these shaping aspects of our culture and examine the ways they've reached into our Sunday services, our youth programs, our conferences, our governance, our approach to God Himself. We hope that the following observations and suggestions help church leaders to become aware of and think critically about those realities. We have, at times, unwittingly wandered into a brand of inconsistency that places God in a secondary position. God does not belong at the periphery; His place is at the center. This is what we mean by putting God in His place.

What We're Doing: Critiques and Constructive Proposals

We are certainly not the first to call attention to the impact of American society on its churches, and we are far from the first to devote study to it. Many scholars and theologians have ably gone before us in this task, from Reinhold Niebuhr and his paradigm-setting models for interaction between Christ and culture to Albert Borgmann's invaluable musings on technology and Christianity. We are deeply indebted to them and their work, and we hope we are able to build upon such thoughtful insight. But our essays are not purely theological, nor are they intended to be scholarly. Instead, we hope to engage those ideas on a level suited for lay readers. Two of us are pastors, and the other two are laymen who serve in our local churches. It is for such people that we intend our book — for pastors and lay leaders, the people who spend year after year devoting themselves to the work of their congregations, the people who make church run. We want to connect the abstract work of cultural criticism with the practical concerns of leading a ministry in such everyday activities as planning worship services, running youth ministries, and engaging in community outreach.

There are plenty of Christians in our generation — people in their twenties and thirties — taking shots at the church, but their solutions are primarily reconstitutions of warmed-over theological liberalism. They identify the problems with today's church and conclude that the problem must be an overdependence on the Bible and rigid theology, so their solution is to rid themselves of both. We identify those problems and conclude the opposite; our shortcomings are precisely because we are not committed enough to the Bible and dedicated to ensuring that our theology flows faithfully from it. These critics are seeing many of the same problems we are, but what they interpret as biblical Christianity is in fact an expression of Christianity taken hostage by the subtle forces of our culture — one bent on the exaltation of the individual.

Likewise, many church leaders are being told that if they are to connect with our generation, they must use an abundance of visual media, technology, and a more "relevant" message. In actuality, however, many young Christians are thirsting for something not more technologically savvy, but more biblically faithful and thoughtfully crafted.

We offer this book to edify the church and assist in its efforts to glorify God. This is not a church-bashing screed aimed at the American megachurch or emergent church or non-emergent church or anyone else. Much of what follows over the next four chapters is indeed critical; still, we humbly intend it as an honest, fair critique of the church's relationship with these cultural forces, and we pray that it will be received as such. Though each of us has experienced frustration with the problems we're pointing out, our intent is not to be bitter or cynical, but to encourage thoughtful discussion and positive change. Because of that purpose, we consider the final section the crux of our message, for

Introduction

it is there that we offer constructive proposals and a vision of the church toward which we strive.

The four cultural realities on which we will focus are hardly the only ones shaping the American church today. One could just as easily write a book addressing the effects of nationalism, Romanticism, or relativism on the church (and many already have). We write about these particular issues not because they are inherently more important than those just mentioned, but because all four major cultural forces have been so adopted by individuals and the church that they shape the ecclesial world while going largely unnoticed. It is their commonality, normality, acceptability, and prevalence coupled with their power to shape the church that brings them into our crosshairs. No church has gone untouched by these four factors. Readers will note that we've elected not to focus on other issues that are important to contemporary evangelicals, such as postmodernism or the rise of the emergent movement. These are worthwhile discussions, but they are not what we are discussing here. Those areas are already being critically addressed, while the four areas we cover are in fact being uncritically embraced by the church.

Our message is predicated on the understanding that the purpose of the church is to bring glory to God. For the sake of the flow of our argument, we've chosen to give only the briefest rationale for this assertion as an introduction to the first part of our book. For those who wish to delve deeper into that issue, we offer a further explanation in an appendix. We reaffirm this long-held truth as a foundation so that we might have something against which to measure the church's actions and by which to guide our concluding proposals.

We're using two potentially unfamiliar terms to help us communicate our point. We use the term cultural realities for those aspects of our culture that have such gravity that they are inescapable. While our culture has many elements that are widely accepted, most of those can be avoided or altered by specific communities while those communities continue to function normally in broader society. Cultural realities, however, are unavoidable, and to eschew them, if that's truly possible at all, is to abandon participation in society. Second, we've chosen the term third-millennium America instead of twenty-first-century America because we believe it better expresses the uniqueness of the unprecedented cultural era that is now.

The remainder of the book is divided into two parts, the first of which consists of four chapters addressing four cultural realities that are subtly shaping the church in third-millennium America. We are not against technology, democracy, media, or capitalism. As stated earlier, to fully reject these cultural realities is to abandon participation in society, and that's not an option for the church, which is called to persist as a preservative and a redeeming force. First, we'll reflect on how marketplace assumptions migrate from the world of the consumer to the world of the church, causing church leaders to preach and model the Gospel in a diminished manner. Next, we'll see that our American democratic principles nurture selfish impulses and undermine the authority of Scripture and the unity of Christ's body. Third, we'll consider how technology presents a rival Gospel — one that satisfies our cravings for comfort, control, and diversion, all without a need for an understanding of our world. Finally, we'll argue that visual media have made the desire to be entertained a core cultural motivation, which reduces our value of the Word and pushes our fixation on amusement into the church.

The book's second section consists of our constructive proposals, which we offer to churches as practical ways to respond to their current cultural situation. We hope that these ideas will be launching points for further discussion, reflection, and action among readers and their fellow church leaders. Ultimately, we pray that our reflections on these issues and the suggestions that follow will serve

Introduction

as a tool to empower churches to recognize cultural assumptions and,
just as the Apostle Paul did in his sermon on Mars Hill, bring Kingdom
thinking to bear on them to aid in ministry that glorifies God and
furthers His Kingdom.

Part I

The Church and Cultural Assumptions in Third-Millennium America

Because of our love for the church and our desire to edify it, we want to precede our critical consideration of culture and the ecclesial world by affirming and discussing the purpose of the church. For a fuller rendition of this discussion, please refer to the appendix.

Some believe that the church has replaced the nation of Israel in God's plan, and others believe that the church is a new addition to the story. But all will agree that the New Testament church has now come to be included among God's people (Acts 15:14). In discerning why the church exists, then, we can take some important cues from Israel, God's covenant people from the Old Testament. Time after time, Scripture records that the result of God's miraculous deliverance for His people is Him receiving honor from both His people and the other inhabitants of the earth. In Numbers 14, where God considers destroying Israel to begin a new people with Moses, Moses' chief argument against such a course is that the Egyptians will perceive it as a failure on God's part.

Perhaps Isaiah 43 states most clearly that God bestowed His love on Israel for His purposes. He redeemed them out of sin and called them to be His people for His glory and His purposes. Even forgiveness of sin was primarily for God's sake. The benefits that the members of His community receive from that forgiveness are secondary to the primary purpose of being purified to be His witnesses (see especially Isa. 43:7-13, 25).

PUTTING GOD IN HIS PLACE

The same is true of the New Testament community of God's people: God is at the center of the story, after all, and not humans. The New Testament writers pick up this theme and repeat it often. Paul tells us that those called into relationship with Him are specifically called to reflect the character of Christ, who just happens to be the perfect image of God (Rom. 8:29, Col. 1:15). In Titus 2:14 he uses language very similar to David, stating simply that God has redeemed and purified a people for His purposes (2 Sam. 7:23). John records Jesus telling His disciples that those who follow Him are to bear fruit for the Father's glory (John 15:8). Peter also affirms that the New Testament community is a new type of spiritual "nation" without boundaries or ethnicities, meant to declare the works and character of God (1 Pet. 2:4, 9-10). Three times in Ephesians 1 Paul emphasizes the idea that the New Testament community has been called and blessed toward the end of glorifying God (Eph. 1:6, 12, 14).

In much the same vein as the Old Testament community of faith, the New Testament community has been assembled for the purpose of being a witness to the character, nature, and works of God. The New Testament church does not exist for itself, but for God's purposes, to be a witnessing community that goes out into the earth and truthfully "images" the true Creator.

The church exists to glorify God. Our next chapters will highlight how four cultural realities in third-millennium America work against Christians and compromise our success in glorifying God. By default we will exalt either ourselves or God. No one can serve two masters (Matt. 6:24).

18

Chapter 1

The Marketplace

By Matt Whitman

You've heard all the maxims from the marketplace and so
have I. The customer is always right. You get what you pay for. Sex
sells. She's moving a lot of product; she must be doing something
right. There are dozens more. These are the sorts of little truisms that
we hear, repeat and rarely question. We are as certain of these rules of
buying and selling as we are of anything. We don't doubt them because
we've seen them proven true again and again; we have countless first
hand encounters to reassure us of their veracity. In third-millennium
America, we all function as accidental scientists conducting endless
daily experiments that reaffirm the maxims of the marketplace again and
again as we buy and sell, and produce and receive marketing messages.
Apart from the most basic laws of physics (like gravity), what are we
more certain of as a result of personal experience than the maxims of
the marketplace? When a culture is as defined by commerce as ours is,
these maxims become unintentional governing life principles.

When church leaders and church attendees go to their place of
worship, they will be hard-pressed to leave at the door the assumptions
that are firmly reinforced the other six days of the week. Americans
spend a lot of time at market. With the advent of internet shopping,
we're even at market when we're at home. It's not just that we seek
out the market, either. Marketing invades our space, and we usually

don't complain. Apart from ideological countermeasures and careful reflection, the assumptions cemented repeatedly by the activities of six-sevenths of one's life will surely inform the assumptions of the other one-seventh. To put it more simply: Consumerism and marketing shape the church in ways we rarely notice.

My intention in this chapter isn't to offer a study of the Christian marketplace. There is plenty of overt overlap between the world of money and the world of church. I'm more interested in considering how the values, beliefs, and assumptions of laypeople and church leaders are molded by their encounters with the marketplace, and how those values, beliefs, and assumptions inform attitudes toward God, church, and the Bible. The marketplace's subtle influence on the church isn't all bad. It isn't all good. It is complicated. In the following pages I'll point out several maxims from the marketplace that inform American Christian faith, and conclude by suggesting distinctions between the governing assumptions of the marketplace and the governing assumptions of Christianity.

I also need to mention that this is not intended to be an anti-capitalism chapter. Rather than debating whether our economic system is best, I want to acknowledge that it's what we've got and that it's overwhelmingly influential whether we find it agreeable or not. My desire is to treat capitalism as a value-neutral cultural expression that has unintended and possibly problematic by-products.

The Customer is Always Right

Savvy business owners understand that it's many times more expensive to gain new customers than it is to retain existing customers. This reality undergirds the maxim from the marketplace that the customer is always right. Of course, "right" is used loosely. In this context "right" means that which yields financial gain, and, since the customer holds the keys to financial gain for the seller, the only definition of truth that matters in a transaction is truth as conceived of by the buyer. It isn't that the consumers have a unique understanding of the universe as it truly is, but rather that vendors can't afford to express disagreement with them. On one level, "the customer is always right" is nothing more than good customer service articulated in a light-hearted manner. However, as consumers become accustomed to this sort of treatment and vendors become accustomed to giving it, both parties can stumble into embracing the crass notion that truth and reality are determined by those who sign the checks.

We're all customers. We're used to a certain kind of treatment. We're used to being told yes. What happens when we come together at church to worship an all-powerful God who commands obedience and submission? Something has to give. This tension can be resolved in a handful of ways. Here are the three options that seem most likely when we bring our marketplace assumptions to church. One option is that we can avoid biblical and theological thought so that no disagreement on such subjects is likely to arise. If there is no disagreement, then no one has to be told no or be made to feel wrong. This second response is the product of a slightly more acute awareness of our attempt to reconcile our marketplace assumptions with our faith. At this point, we may recast God as a supernatural agent of our temporal satisfaction. We expect Him to give us what we desire on our terms. A third response is to shop. We select those aspects of who God is or what He has revealed that are compatible with our lifestyles and assumptions and disregard those that aren't — sort of like ordering at Burger King, where you can "have it your way."

After All, You Deserve It

In order for a marketer to convince a potential customer to part ways with her hard-earned money, he must overcome a number of potential objections. Perhaps the target of his marketing has an aversion to debt, is loyal to a different brand, isn't aware of a deficiency in her life that could be addressed with his product, or feels guilt about spending money on personal indulgence. Of course, there are techniques marketers use to challenge each of these objections. One such technique is to market with the rationale that the consumer "deserves it" or "has earned it." Advertisements consistently remind us that we do so much for others, that we work so hard, or that we deny ourselves the little things so often that it would not only be okay to indulge, but it would be foolish not to. Though we may feel underappreciated by those around us, we never have to question whether or not advertisers understand and appreciate all of our hard work; they certainly do and they want us to know it.

Advertising isn't the only place where our self-esteem is edified. We live in a society that values self-confidence and feeling good about ourselves. I'm thankful we don't feel a constant social obligation to degrade ourselves and feel worthless — there are mental, relational, and physical health benefits to having a healthy self-image. However, I again wonder how compatible this maxim of the marketplace is with Christian faith and the purpose of the church. The Scriptures teach that we gain a sense of identity in Christ (2 Cor. 5:17-19) and that we are created in God's image (Gen. 1:27). These are things that should cause us to feel good about ourselves, though we must admit that these aren't things accomplished by our own merit. We are the beneficiaries of God demonstrating His glory by creating us, by lavishing His love on us, and by giving us a new sense of self and a new destiny in Christ. The ultimate reward isn't earned. We're not entitled to heaven because we do so much for others, or work so hard, or constantly deny ourselves. We're entitled because of Christ's righteousness and God's merciful efforts (Rom. 3:21-26). In this respect, the message of the Bible differs from the marketer's alluring expressions of appreciation for our merits.

Assumptions of entitlement run contrary to Christian teaching, but we bring these assumptions with us to church. Christians may feel entitled to being constantly served by their church instead of constantly serving with their church because "after all, we deserve it." We may also feel that church should be catered to our tastes and interests for the same reasons. Churchgoers might walk out of the morning service expressing concern that the musical style of the worship wasn't in keeping with their preferences, while giving little thought to whether the time of worship was glorifying to God. When this marketing technique evolves in our thinking from a selling point to an attitude toward life, we may forget that the church exists for the glory of God and make the mistake of thinking church exists for our personal satisfaction. Our conduct as church attendees or as church leaders is affected dramatically by whether we assume church is first and foremost about us, the consumer, or whether we believe it to be about the glory of God. If church is about us, then the driving question must be, "Am I satisfied with how this works for me?" If church is about God and His glory, then a better question might be, "Regardless of whether I personally like it or not, is God glorified by who we are and what we are doing?"

You've Got to Get Your Message Out

So you've come up with a great product. Well, unless you find a way to let the world know, it counts for nothing. If you want to succeed in business, people have to know that your business is there and what it's about. If you want to succeed in your job search, you have to find a way to get potential employers' attention and let them know why you're the one they should hire. Even the best product in the world doesn't sell itself; you've got to get your message out.

That's hard to argue with, but the act of communicating a message itself is loaded with meaning. What do the tactics we use to get our message out convey on the unspoken level? This question may not be that important of a consideration in the realm of business and commerce, but if we assume that churches and individual Christians ought to "get their message out," then the question is a very important one for us. After all, we want to get our message right and we certainly don't want to send a mixed message or have our message compromised by how we communicate it. Again, "you've got to get your message out" is a maxim from the marketplace that has numerous consequences when applied the Christian life and to church.

First, and most usefully, it can remind Christians to proclaim the Gospel and the glory of God. In theory, the testimony of Scripture should be enough to prompt this, but extra-biblical trends that remind us to do expressly biblical things are good and helpful too. After this general point, however, things can become more problematic.

A second expression of getting our message out is branding. A brand is a way to distinguish very similar products from one another. Good branding involves attaching a story to a product that connects a set of desirable attributes to it. Consider the recent television marketing campaigns for the Toyota Tundra. In an attempt to overcome their image as specializing in small efficient sedans, and to combat the idea that buying a Toyota is un-American, Tundra commercials have taken a decidedly rural American tone. They hired a voice actor with a gravelly drawl and a practical, blue-collar tone to voice over images of Tundras at Fourth of July celebrations, rodeos, and softball games. Whereas showing Tundras parked outside anime conventions or being used to pick up a batch of school girls wearing Hello Kitty backpacks would only serve to reinforce an old brand that they're trying to get away from, the Americana images are intended to make consumers attach a whole new set of images and associations to the truck. The truck hasn't changed just because Toyota hired Sam Elliot to read the advertisement instead of Ichiro Suzuki.

Many churches are going through a period of rebranding right now; trying to unload stuffy images of preachers in suits, old people, and all things hierarchical, and replace them with images of relevant speakers, hip young people, and all things iGeneration. They want to convey that church isn't about rules, obligations, or the past; it's about your story and God's story. Consultants ask church boards to consider what makes their church unique; distinctive from the church down the road, and then run with that message. In the same way that Toyota nurtures its brand power, so many churches handle their brand with great thoughtfulness and care to make sure that they are getting their message out. But, if what we mean by "message" is the Gospel and God's glory, is this type of branding really serving to "get the message out" or does it obscure the message? Does branding accomplish anything more than serving to build each individual church institution? If Toyota needs to alter our perceptions for the sake of sales, maybe that's fine, but as the church we should be cautious about following suit, lest we compromise the power and substance of the Gospel by retooling the message and our image to work people into having the perception of us that we want.

Build a Better Mousetrap

If you want to get ahead, build a better mousetrap. That's a paraphrase of a paraphrase of how the free market works for the entrepreneurial. All you have to do to be successful is put out a better product (and get your message out) and the customers will choose it. In this respect, the market polices itself. It purges itself of inferior products in favor of better and better things. Even though the government intervenes in the market from time to time, for the most part, we're sold on this idea.

However, if we bring this maxim from the marketplace to bear on church, we run the risk of developing rivalries with other churches instead of rooting for and praying for other ambassadors of Christ and His Kingdom. Would the Kingdom really benefit if a handful of churches with tremendous resources siphoned off Christians from smaller churches because of the allure of superior programming and facilities? In Scripture, God demonstrates His propensity for using unimpressive people (by cultural standards) to accomplish His purposes (i.e. Ex. 4:10, Josh. 2, Num. 22:1-35). We apply the "market will police itself" maxim to the church at our own peril and at the peril of the Kingdom. Many resources are squandered as churches try to out-church their rivals instead of promoting the Kingdom and proclaiming God's glory. This type of thinking is akin to ecclesiastical Darwinism — that is, the callous notion that the fittest local churches will survive and churches that wane or expire can be dismissed as having been unfit.

We'll discuss this topic further and offer constructive suggestions in the second part of the book, but until then, I'll emphasize that what I mean is not that churches shouldn't strive for excellence (I'm writing this chapter because I believe we should strive for excellence). Rather, we should strive for excellence because it brings glory to God and not because excellence will advance our institution over others.

They're Moving a Lot of Product. They Must Be Doing Something Right

This maxim from the marketplace is little more than economic pragmatism. The idea here is that where there are good results, the process must be (at least in part) right. If the maxim is true, observers are obligated to acknowledge that successful practices can't be all wrong because they've yielded tangible results, even if observers might find parts of the successful business's approach to be objectionable. This mentality presents a moral question that members of the marketplace may wrestle with. Is success merely defined by financial gain, or is propriety in the process part of what defines success? If it's all about financial gain, then factors determining the quality of a business might include the size of the business' facilities, the number of countries in which a product is sold, awards presented to honor a business or product, popularity of a business or product, the brand power of a business or product, or the total amount of money earned. If the process matters, then all of those accolades could be diminished if the means by which they were achieved is dubious.

As it pertains to church, this maxim may have a different effect depending on certain theological assumptions. If one believes that wealthy or well-attended churches can only be so because of the direct blessing of God, then that individual is likely to assume that the spiritual health and ministry philosophy espoused by leaders of a successful church must be right. After all, "They're reaching a lot of people and they're doing another building project. They must be doing something right!" If one believes that churches could demonstrate outward signs of health without fulfilling the purpose of the church, he or she is not obligated to assume that all good-looking churches are doing something right (Matt 23:27).

Regardless of theological persuasion, the most obvious risk of this maxim when thoughtlessly applied to church is that we will use non-biblical and false measurements to determine success at the expense of the measurements we're actually supposed to be using. We may be tempted to measure success based on size, wealth, facilities, the attractiveness of the people who come, the neighborhood in which the church is built, the amount of Christian product we're able to sell within the church, the opinions of the cultural elite, or the stylishness of our music and services in general (1 Sam. 16:7). If, for example, the sole objective of church is to be big, there are many steps we could take to achieve this. We could have vendors distribute free nachos and beer during the message. We could hand out free money to thank people for coming. We could have a sweepstakes every week where one lucky family wins a trip to Disneyland. We could sexualize our content. These all might make us bigger, but surely, we'd agree that these are all very problematic avenues to growth. Those are absurd examples, but the point is that if growth is the number one measure of success, there are many ways we could achieve that end that don't glorify God's name or serve the purposes of His Kingdom.

If we measure things the wrong way, we'll celebrate the wrong things. If we celebrate certain predetermined outcomes and disregard the process, we may falsely achieve "success" while actually accomplishing nothing, or worse, blatantly sinning. If outcomes are all that matters, we lose the ability to faithfully serve, whether God has chosen to bless or chosen not to (Dan. 3:17-18). Showing up and doing church, even in the most biblical of manners, does not come with the promise that God who wasn't in the wind, fire, or earthquake will supernaturally intervene and make our church big and influential.

Sex Sells

Obviously, advertisers have determined that attractive people doing sexually charged things are attention-getters. This isn't a recent discovery. A two-minute, four-commercial break may include one ad that expressly uses sexuality or even sexual imagery to help sell a product, but that doesn't mean the other three ads aren't operating in keeping with the maxim from the marketplace that sex sells. Advertisements portray a sexier version of reality — a possibility, perhaps, but more so an ideal notion of a product, person, or situation. In some ways advertisements present the marketing equivalent of a platonic universal. In this imagined world of perfection there isn't room for the old, fat, bald, blemished, poor, or dull. Why would anyone part with their money to acquire something so undesirable — something they could easily have for free? Selling with sex is about more than skin; it's about a potential sexier version of you and your reality.

There are churches and leaders who are moving away from what they consider to be prudish reads on sexuality and church, but it appears to me that this is still a minority group. Of course this is difficult to quantify, but it seems that most churches and church leaders still bristle at the idea of selling Jesus by appealing to sexual desires. However, as with each of these examples, the overt is rarely the problem; it is the unintentional way in which each of these maxims shapes our thinking that is of greatest concern. This is evident in many of the worship songs we sing in churches that present Jesus in the language of a teenage crush.

Most adults, be they Christians or otherwise, are discerning enough to know that marketing is not a reliable source of truth. We all know that it would be foolish to take the words of advertisers at face value. But it's harder to keep from having our ideals shaped by a continual series of messages all affirming the same set of values. Advertisers are constantly laboring to redefine reality. Maybe few leaders would deliberately parade out a sexually attractive female dressed to accentuate her best features just so that people will perk up for worship, but we might succumb to the muted pressure to present an idealized version of people in church to match cultural expectations for what goodness and success look like. It may be fine to trot out our youngest, hippest, and most attractive every Sunday morning, but then again it may not be. Might that dedication to what culture deems attractive or desirable alienate marginalized people, or possibly even average people? We might suppose that a church needs to have that "sexy" look to validate its message the same way that we feel more comfortable going to a car dealership that is clean and staffed by reputable down-to-earth-looking people. Showing preference to good-looking people when deciding who we'll ask to be the face of the church may cause church to be one more place that adds to the constant pressure applied to a culture convinced of the "sex sells" maxim. A wink-wink employment of sex to help sell our messages at church may also create an obsession with youth and cause us to disparage older people and older ideas. Since we're very dependent on the resurrection (which is a 2,000-year-old event) we might be cutting off our nose to spite our face if we nurture disregard for things old in favor using youth to sell our message and our institutions.

Because we can't help how people look, or what some will find attractive, this may be difficult to address meaningfully. Even if that's the case, we should be aware of this maxim and consider how it might be shaping our assumptions as Christian leaders and as churchgoers.

You Get What You Pay For

Several of these maxims have been from the perspective of the marketer or the free market theorist, but the maxim "you get what you pay for" is one spoken most by the consumer. This is a statement of resignation that acknowledges that to spare expense is to spare quality. When applied to church and Christian thought, this idea can skew our judgment on what a viable ministry might look like. Might we pay more attention to a message preached in a new sanctuary, than the same message preached in a building in ill repair? Might we discount the significance of the non-Western church because it runs on a smaller budget? Might we be tempted to spend more money just to look more legitimate? Is there room for poor churches in a wealthy society?

If we accept that the exchange of money for goods and services is one of the most common aspects of human relations in our culture, then we must consider how that interaction might inform how people think about church. It is only natural that we might think of church and salvation as a transaction in which congregants give church their money and attendance in exchange for the church's proclamation of salvation upon them. And if it is to be conceived of as a transaction, and one isn't attending an impressive church, perhaps they might fear that they're receiving a diminished version of salvation or a reduced relationship with God. After all, you get what you pay for.

Sit Back, Relax, and Enjoy the Show

You've put in a long day of work, you've dropped the kids off at the baby sitter, you've battled traffic, and you've finally landed in a seat at the theater. Whether a host strolls out onto the stage and says the actual words or not, the message is clear, "Sit back, relax, and enjoy the show." Nothing is expected of you. Things are expected of you at work and at home, but you've set up these two hours and paid good money so that you don't have to think about your responsibilities or fear being called upon to do something. You are anonymous and that's something you had to sacrifice to achieve. Even if going out is unrealistic, the television offers some of the same. Consumers buy this kind of brief escape and, as paying customers, expect their purchase to be honored.

Why not carry over the assumptions from the movie theater or the concert hall to the church? It looks similar. The format is similar. If we give money, we might even feel the sense of entitlement to encounter it on our terms that we do as a paying customer at the movies. Purchase seems to give us the impression that we are entitled to passivity. In church that can translate to the idea that we can "outsource" our faith to the hired spiritual elite who think Christian thoughts and do Christian things on our behalf. Being engaged in a voluntary organization like church and serving as an agent of God's Kingdom and herald of His glory aren't ideas that mesh well with our cultural belief in purchasing the privilege of passivity.

The First Time's Free, Even for a Chump Like You

I heard this expression in an after-school special during my pre-teen years. It was one of my first encounters with a portrayal of drug use and teen drug culture. Of course the special was demonstrating how the "pusher" was giving away an expensive street drug to a conflicted young person with the intent of getting her hooked and then changing the rules. Sure enough, the kid got addicted, but all of a sudden, the drugs stopped being free. The drug got hyped and sold without the aspiring addict being given the chance to really add up just how much her new habit was going to cost her over the long run. The dealer deliberately withheld all that information, because he rightly knew that disclosing such things would reduce the likelihood of the young girl saying yes the first time.

Maybe you see where I'm going with this. How often do church leaders get together with other church leaders and lament the lack of commitment and resistance to obey God demonstrated by congregants at their churches? I've heard the expression "a mile wide and an inch deep" many times from many different pastors. Why? Perhaps we have been informed by marketers' (not just drug dealers, either) tendency to withhold any information that is a strike against purchasing their product, and we too feel the need to sweeten the deal as Christians sharing the Gospel. Marketers know their products well, and they've tried to sell it enough times to know what the common sticking points are. If they can find a way to avoid those sticking points, they'll be much more successful. Christians who've shared the Gospel either know by experience or suppose to know the sticking points for people when hearing about salvation. Avoiding those sticking points is a natural but problematic thing to do (although Christ never felt compelled to avoid them). If the Gospel invitation is to believe in Jesus and then go to heaven, that's a relatively easy sell with almost no imaginable sticking points. However, if the invitation also involves language of submission to God, obedience to His commands, commitment to service, being crucified with Christ, and dying to self, there are a few more things that a potential convert might get hung up on. If we embrace the softer version of the Gospel there isn't much cost to be counted — conversion is a no-brainer. However, Christ calls believers to much more. He doesn't just offer or pitch salvation; He commands repentance.

Though few pastors or lay leaders would suggest that watering down the Gospel is a good idea, we still fall victim to the desire to sell a lot of anything instead of a possibly more measured amount of the right thing. We might soften the Gospel because theologically we believe we bear the primary responsibility for its success and feel that telling a potential convert the whole thing right up front might damage our chances of fulfilling our own obligation to make disciples. We might soften it accidentally as we instinctively feel out the consumers and try to be sensitive to their needs. The usually unintentional bait and switch backfires, however, when we realize that we've won converts to a religion that doesn't involve anything other than an attachment to Jesus after the conversion encounter. We may be tempted to blame immature Christians for their thick-headedness and resistance to growth, but before we do, we might consider whether they ever actually agreed to be followers of Christ as revealed in the Scriptures, and what amount of responsibility we might bear for that possible shortcoming.

Buyer Beware: Concluding Thoughts

In a society where we are not only invited to fully participate in the market, but in fact the welfare of the economic system depends on our participation, we must realize that our understanding of self, church, and God will all be sculpted by the realities of the marketplace. We cannot help but be shaped by these maxims. It is understandable that what seems so true and logical in the marketplace would be just as true and applicable in church, but there are several distinctions between the two that require them to be governed by different principles.

First, the free market is a cold, impersonal, artificial entity. We give it a personality and animated qualities, but it isn't alive, it isn't real, and it certainly has no feelings for individuals or groups of people. It is nonsensical to bring the tendencies and assumptions gained from interacting with this impersonal entity into an environment meant for interaction with and the glorification of a God who emptied Himself and made Himself nothing to take on personal human form. Approaching Him and His church as though we were interacting with the market is, in a sense, to deny His incarnation.

Second, the free market is predicated on the idea that a reasonable measure of selfishness on the part of all participants will result in a tension that will benefit everyone involved, regardless of their economic position. Christ calls us to yield our rights, hold loosely to our possessions, and store up lasting treasures in heaven. We may need to participate in the free market as Christians to eat and provide for our families, but we aren't obligated to take market assumptions to church with us, let alone allow those assumptions to trump Christ's commands.

Third, the market is concerned with outputs and the net result of our efforts. Christ is concerned with obedience and love for Him. Those are difficult things to measure in terms of tangible outputs.

Fourth, in a free market, merit largely determines our standing. We earn things by hard work and ingenuity, and then we are entitled to reap the rewards. As followers of Christ, dependence on our own merit is a sure path to condemnation. We are entitled to nothing but the promises of Christ made possible by His mercy enacted in His work on the cross and in the resurrection. A position of humble gratitude, not a position of well-earned entitlement, is the only position that makes sense given the way we are saved.

This is not intended to be an anti-capitalistic chapter. Capitalism may be the economic system that is most conducive to Christian living and widespread cultural virtue. However, our market and our God are very different things, and we often fail to notice that distinction as we syncretize our faith in the maxims of our market with our faith in Christ.

Chapter 2

Democracy and Individualism

By Aron Utecht

We are a nation of individuals. And while that might seem obvious, that simple fact of life in third-millennium America has had a profound impact on how we approach and practice our faith in our cultural setting. We believe in democracy. We believe in the dignity of the individual. We affirm the rights of the individual. We believe that each of us has ideas to contribute for the benefit of all. We believe that human government derives its legitimacy from the consent of the governed.

These ideals are all noble, but how well to do they mesh with the "faith, once for all handed down to the saints" (Jude 3)? In good and bad ways, our democratic and individualistic assumptions have become part of the way that Christians live out their faith in third-millennium America.

Like all Christians of every age, we live in human culture. As we try to influence our environment, it also places its imprint on us. It is unavoidable, and to deny it is foolish. I put forward here my observations as one who also lives in third-millennium America, participating in its institutions, embedded in its pop culture and enjoying its freedoms and conveniences. I'll first offer a survey of our democratic processes and the values that go with it. Following that background, I'll demonstrate how these democratic and individualistic assumptions have influenced negatively how many Christians live out their faith.

Our Democratic Assumptions

One democratic philosophy that has been with us since our founding is social contract theory. The principal idea is that the individual sacrifices some of her personal freedom to join herself to a larger body. By joining together and sacrificing a small level of autonomy each member actually experiences more benefits and freedom. The community joins itself together with a governing document or agreement — a constitution in our case — and that becomes the basis for authority. The members, either directly or through representatives, ratify the document, and all pledge to live by it.

One of the benefits to this arrangement is that power is shared by all. Those chosen to enforce the contract or constitution come from among those who have willingly submitted to it. The office they hold is not above the governing document, and it, not they, is the final arbiter of what is acceptable among the community. The governing document also has the benefit of being transparent and objective. Under such a document, all members of the community know what is acceptable, and if there is a dispute or a member out of line the correction is not derived from the whim of an individual. Ideally, a social contract provides a check on individualism by bringing individuals together.

One way in which our culture has worked out this contract is the separation of powers. Even with a guiding document, it was acknowledged that too much power in the hands of one individual would give that person an unfair influence. The assumption is that a person with too much authority should not be trusted. Power corrupts. Too much power in one person's hands ruins that individual, as human history has amply shown. A separation of power is good for the community and good for the individual. Democracy has an automatic suspicion of authority built into the system. Given our fallen natures, this seems to serve the cause of good governance well, but it brings some complications when applied to the church, as I'll illustrate shortly.

Democracy and Individualism

The key mechanism in a social contract is voluntary association. For virtually all of our history, Americans have formed and participated in clubs and organizations of all stripes. Each of these reflects the spirit, if not the formal structure, of a social contract where the individuals join ranks to advance their cause.

The key player in the social contract is the individual. She can choose to participate in any social organization that she wishes, or choose none at all. And if she doesn't like the social contract she's bound to, she has the option to join with other like-minded members of the community to get it changed. Our "one person, one vote" ideal enables this arrangement.

Likewise, consider these famous words from the Declaration of Independence: "We hold these truths to be self-evident that all men are created equal, and are endowed by their creator with certain unalienable rights. Among these are life, liberty and the pursuit of happiness." The ultimate end of all our freedom is the personal fulfillment of the individual. Our social contract — the Constitution — and its accompanying institutions are designed to protect and further three things: life, personal autonomy, and personal fulfillment.

The idea that all men are created equal was radical in 1776, though it is a commonplace idea today. The value contained in this principle is that each person is to be regarded equally and treated fairly under the law. In time this cultural belief birthed its own offspring. The principle that all people are created equal has evolved into the belief that all people's ideas are, in theory at least, equally valid and should have a hearing. The way we interpret this is, "My ideas are as valid as anyone else's and deserve to be heard." All ideas are judged on their merits. In principle this is very good; it can result in people being more involved in the process of determining the direction of the community. In an environment of healthy, rational discourse where opposing factions will weigh the merits of a particular viewpoint and are willing to be persuaded, genuine consensus is achieved. In this ideal, the best of both viewpoints would yield not only a compromise, but also something better than each side could develop on its own.

Of course, in reality, not all ideas are equal. Some are good, some are better, and some are just plain dreadful. But in the ideal setting, where disparate parties are willing to reason through issues and be persuaded by a better argument, the lesser ideas are weighed and found wanting. What is "right" or "true" is reached by reason and compromise in the best interest of all. The source for authority becomes the group consensus — the will of the people.

In practice, a genuine consensus isn't always easy to come by. Elitism, where one voice or a collection of voices tries to talk down to the masses, has always been resented to a large degree. The populist mantra, "No one has the right to tell me what to think or believe," is deeply ingrained. This latent anti-intellectualism makes it easy to dismiss other's ideas as too academic, irrelevant, or impractical. Playing the populist card is a shortcut to undermining an opponent's position without having to engage in the more difficult work of weighing its merits.

The American ideal of determining consensus through open dialogue, reasoned discussion and compromise is just that — ideal. Contemporary American culture has fallen far from this ideal (if it was ever truly realized in the first place). In the current climate it has become exceedingly rare to hear anyone acknowledge the merits of an opponent's idea. Instead of a willingness to be persuaded by reason, cultural leaders and opinion shapers are, by and large, committed partisans. Whether the issue is social or political, the usual stance is to undercut opponents by any means necessary. This could include but is not limited to attacking their character, undermining their credibility, or simply shouting them down to keep anyone else from hearing their argument.

Democracy and Individualism

Such tactics and logical fallacies obviously don't build consensus. What takes the place of consensus is majority rule, usually with a disgruntled minority. In this caustic environment, people are not interested in ideas or what is best for all. They are interested in power, because obtaining power is the only way to advance your own ideas and to protect you from the other viewpoint. This yields winners and losers. A compromise and consensus approach allows for people to support the community — the whole. But when a majority is able to enforce its wishes on an unwilling minority, the decision-making process brings division to the community instead of bringing it together.

In third-millennium America, we find ourselves in a situation where our cultural mechanisms and institutions push us apart. Instead of a sense of responsibility toward the common good, we are experiencing the backlash of our individualistic faults. Individuals and groups of individuals clamor for rights, whether it's the right to own guns, the right to a smoke-free society, or the right to choose to end a pregnancy. When majority rule replaces consensus as the source for authority opposing ideas aren't given their hearing. When no one is listening and no one feels heard, the result is the cultural equivalent of every man for himself. From the standpoint of the individual, the only recourse is to defend whatever cultural territory one has left and try not to lose any more ground. Discourse degenerates into politics as war, rather than dialogue for the common good.

In this atmosphere, authority is determined by who has power, regardless of the merit of their ideas; whoever disagrees is marginalized or silenced. These are hardly the tendencies of a healthy, sustainable culture, and not a good mechanism for determining what's real, best and true. But the church is still an institution that professes to care about what's real, best and true. Using the consensus of the people as a source for authority in the church has some shortcomings. Making the will of the majority the determinant for ultimate truth is even more problematic.

These are a few of the ways that we've fallen from our own ideals.

Saving our democratic model is not my goal here, but these factors have shaped the culture we live in today. So far I've tried to simply describe a present cultural reality. Here is how we take a few of these assumptions to church with us.

Democracy and the Church

The democratic approach to life that has made our country unique, and even in some ways great, has accordingly had its influence on church life. These examples are found most clearly among those churches that have adopted a congregational polity, and though more subtle, they're present in other forms of polity too. Here are two ways our democratic impulses have benefited the church.

1. They provide a check on power. If power corrupts, the church is not immune. The decentralized nature of evangelicalism has made it especially susceptible to dynamic personalities that have a little success and then begin building their own kingdom instead of God's. One way that our democratic influences have benefited the church is they provide a check on power in our church structures. This sharing of power among the congregation can be a helpful corrective against a leader who tries to take things in the wrong direction. Even in a church structure that is not explicitly congregational, every pastor and leader knows he must work to get people rallied behind his idea or they will voluntarily dissociate!

2. They promote responsive leadership. Another benefit to a democratic approach is that it forces the leadership to be genuinely responsive to the congregation. It sets up a structure in which the participants have at least a measure of input on the direction of the church. Congregationalism allows members to have a hearing, which prevents the negativity and suspicion that is bred in an environment where participants feel they have no voice. It provides a platform for participants to have access to the leaders and for all to come to consensus together on important issues that affect them all personally. This also has the somewhat unintentional benefit of drawing people together in unity over the process, which also results in a higher commitment level from the congregation. Congregationalism, checks and balances, and a forum for members to be heard are all positive ways in which democratic ideas have been integrated into church.

The Other Side of the Coin

But there is another side, too. Here are some ways that democratic assumptions elevate the individual and infringes on God's rightful place.

1. They promote individualism and self-interest. Though democracy lends some helpful influences to the church, its core assumptions elevate the individual, which poses problems for the body. Individualism runs contrary to Scripture. Paul instructs us in Philippians 2:3-4 to "Do nothing out of selfish ambition or vain conceit, but in humility consider others better than yourselves. Each of you should look not only to your own interests, but also to the interests of others." If the heart of a social contract is the idea that the individual obtains greater liberty by sacrificing a small amount of autonomy, then the individual is ultimately joining for self-serving reasons.

People who join a church for personal benefit will eventually find themselves at odds with Christ. Likewise, churches that present only the privileges of membership to prospective members are unwittingly setting them up for failure. Dietrich Bonhoeffer summed it up well: "When Christ calls a man, He bids him come and die." We are told to give up our own personal agenda. None of us have the right to draw boundaries on the lordship of Christ. We are creatures created by the Creator for His purposes. Whatever Christ asks us to give, it is His right to do so. A social contract is designed to expand the rights of an individual. In our case, we've articulated those as "life, liberty, and the pursuit of happiness." This pursuit of self-interest is antithetical to the message of the cross.

Consider Jesus' teachings: "… anyone who does not take his cross and follow me is not worthy of me. Whoever finds his life will lose it, and whoever loses his life for my sake will find it" (Matt. 10:38-39). "I tell you the truth, unless a kernel of wheat falls to the ground and dies, it remains only a single seed. But if it dies, it produces many seeds. The man who loves his life will lose it, while the man who hates his life in this world will keep it for eternal life" (John 12:24-25). Speaking of his own achievements, Paul has much the same thing to say: "I consider everything a loss compared to the surpassing greatness of knowing Christ Jesus my Lord, for whose sake I have lost all things" (Phil. 3:8).

As church leaders we will have a hard time challenging people's deep-seated assumptions. But we do ourselves no good in appealing to those assumptions. We would do far better to speak frankly to our congregations and potential converts, expecting them to join our faith and our church because it is true and right. We should disclose candidly at the outset of our interaction that joining us, and following our Savior might bring greater difficulty than their current status (at least for this present life). Part of the message of the New Testament is that following Christ means taking a difficult road for this life (see Matt. 10:17-25; John 16:33; 1 Thess. 3:1-5; 2 Tim. 3:12; 1 Pet. 3-5).

The same truth also relates to recruiting volunteers. Our cultural assumptions tell us that participating is in our self-interest. Only the most mature people serve for unselfish reasons. Perhaps this is one reason why recruiting volunteers is difficult. Altruism is a value that is rarely nurtured culturally, so we end up trying to convince people it's in their best interest to serve, rather than just explaining that God commands them to give of their time, talent, and treasure.

2. They encourage a competing authority. The democratic process is designed to determine the will of the people. The consensus of the community then becomes the authority, and guiding force — the working definition of truth. This approach to authority is problematic when applied to the Christian faith.

Regrettably, the distinction between the will of the people and the will of God can easily be lost. In committee or congregational meetings that feel just like any other board or town hall meeting, it takes an intentional mindset to remember that it is God's wishes that are being sought after, and not the community's. In a body where the solid majority of individuals are thoroughly grounded in the Scriptures and doctrine, the system works. But where a congregation is not as tied to or well versed in God's Word, there is no internal mechanism to ensure that the consensus actually reflects scriptural teaching.

There are the horror stories that get retold in seminaries about pastors coming home from a trip to find they've been dismissed, or the business meeting that devolves into a fight over some decorating decision for the new addition. Thankfully, these are extreme examples of congregationalism gone awry. More typically, when congregationalism fails, the result is a church that is lacking in vision and leadership gradually sliding into institutional self-preservation rather than taking risks for God's Kingdom.

3. They nurture a resistance to authority. The worst of our populist impulses have the potential to exacerbate this problem. Populism resists intellectual authorities. In the church, the intellectual authorities are also the spiritual authorities. It is a dangerous combination when a community of believers 1) is not grounded doctrinally and 2) flirts with the idea that it is offensive for someone to tell them something they haven't discovered on their own. Resisting spiritual authorities (usually pastors and elders) is not just problematic, it is sinful (see 1 Tim. 4:12, 5:17-21; esp. Heb. 13:17). Even Martin

PUTTING GOD IN HIS PLACE

Luther began the Reformation as a monk committed to the system and authorities he lived under. It was only when those authorities refused to listen to the voice of Scripture that he finally separated. The writer of Hebrews exhorts us to submit to our spiritual authorities. That is a very difficult concept to follow if one subconsciously likens their leaders to elected representatives. It might not always result in a drive to "recall" a leader, but it allows a sinful root of bitterness to fester.

This represents our suspicion of authority at work. Ingrained in our American psyche is a subtle distrust of those in authority that can flare up at any time. That dogma deserves to be challenged. There are examples of ministers who have taken advantage of their congregations, but the vast majority of men and women leading in churches are serving well. It is unfortunate when we don't realize our natural cultural bias against them.

It would be rare for this bias to result in open rebellion. It's more likely to result in the minister being treated like an employee who is answerable to the board. The underlying attitude is that it's the congregation's church and not the pastor's, so he has less invested in the institution. Most pastors or staff members, however, have as much or more invested in seeing the organization thrive, since it is where they spend the best hours of their day (and too often nights too!). The conventional wisdom is that it is the congregation's church, and a staff member can always relocate to another church. Yet any church leader will tell you that paid staff have no monopoly on leaving and finding new churches! Moreover, that kind of attitude would only encourage staff to keep moving on, contributing to the short cycles of hire/rehire that are the norm for many large churches now.

Treating spiritual authorities like paid employees can make pastoral ministry very difficult. Teaching the whole council of God necessarily includes some difficult material; how to handle money and business dealings, or how we should treat our spouse and kids, or the fact that God really doesn't want us to have sex outside of marriage are all difficult messages to hear. Everybody in the room can feel the tension when those things come up. Knowing (if even subconsciously) that the church is a volunteer organization and that anyone who tells people things they don't want to hear risks running people off makes preaching a tough balancing act.

This isn't the really hard stuff, either. If a pastor has to lead the church in a truly challenging direction, he can only push so far before the question arises as to who really has the power and right to set the direction and values of the church. Moving the congregation away from institutional self-preservation and country-club thinking toward a mission/sacrifice mentality can be tough because it runs against not only our sin nature, but also against many of our cultural values.

Church discipline can be extremely difficult in a context where self-interest is nurtured instead of being expressly called out. The minister understands that he must answer to the congregation, yet he also knows that God has made His standard very clear, and it is the pastor's job to relay that. He is in the unenviable position of rebuking those to whom he is answerable. We are all ultimately answerable to God, but that does not make it any easier to bite the hand that feeds us. As I've already pointed out, submission to spiritual authorities is not generally congruent with a democratic approach to church. If the individual or family being corrected has power, they can make it difficult for the pastor trying to exhort to holiness. More often than not, the individuals being challenged will simply leave. In either case, the goal of bringing God's people to holiness is thwarted.

People might leave for other reasons, too. If they are unhappy about the pastor's preaching, didn't get their way over a building project, or any other number of things, it is possible to go find another fellowship — or drag those sympathetic to their issue off with them and just create their own new church (or new denomination even!). In this particular type of social contract, the participants are not bound by geographical or national concerns; they simply withdraw from participation. The result is that offenses among Christ's church go unresolved, and the unity that Christ prayed for in John 17 is mocked. It is the spiritual equivalent of "play by my rules or I'm taking my ball and going home."

Such conduct is nurtured and often given a pass in a society where the main actor is the individual. As members of Christ's church, like our entire culture, we conceive of ourselves as a group of individuals rather than a community. Loyalty to self trumps our loyalty to all voluntary associations, including the church. This thinking leaves little room for submitting ourselves to each other in Christ (Eph. 5:21). Jesus and the New Testament authors are very clear that our loyalty to Christ and then His community should supersede our personal agendas.

4. They misrepresent the Gospel. This individualism, in turn, both affirms and informs our popular notion of what the Gospel is. To a large extent, our American cultural assumptions lead us to believe that the Gospel is about our own personal fulfillment. It's not often that an evangelical preacher would minimize sin and the need for conversion. But if that essential, life-saving message is wrapped in language of personal peace our offense to the holiness of God can be minimized. We have learned that a command to repent doesn't get the same response as an offer of heaven, and that has shaped our message. We invite people to make a personal decision, rather than join the community of disciples.

As Americans, we are a nation of individuals. Because of this it is most natural for us to think and act in our in our own self-interest. Unfortunately, this thinking doesn't stay home on Sundays. Our cultural values and system of governance provide for many blessings and freedoms. People are treated with dignity, and following Christ openly and boldly rarely brings serious consequences. Yet our fallen natures don't usually handle such liberty too well. Not only do our democratic

Democracy and Individualism

notions of freedom and individuality run against the grain of Christian
community, they can too often make it less distinctively Christian.

Speaking of democracy, well-known New Testament Scholar
D.A. Carson notes that it has many benefits. He writes, "But it has
also proved proficient at throwing off a sense of obligation to God
the Creator, let alone the God and Father of our Lord Jesus Christ,
which is another way of saying it is proficient at fostering idolatry."
Along with its many praiseworthy freedoms, Carson observes there is
also "the freedom to be a hedonist, to pursue a life revolving around
entertainment, to become inured against responsible family life,
communal interaction, and self-denying service in the endless worship
of massive egos, passing fads, and this-worldly glitter."

A friend of mine likes to point out that what you win people
with, you win them to. Tapping into people's self-serving instincts is
ultimately antithetical to genuine discipleship. Relying on our cultural
assumptions instead of challenging them is the wrong starting point for a
life of submission to Christ.

Chapter 3

Technology

By Matt Ostercamp

Technology is not new. Genesis 4 tells us that Tubal-Cain forged all kinds of tools out of bronze and iron. The making and using of tools has never ceased since. What is new as we enter the third millennium after Christ is the rapid evolution of our technology, the magnitude of our technologically enhanced power and the pervasiveness of the technological filter through which we experience the world. Reality is mediated in contemporary America through technology. We stay in touch with our community by watching news on television or reading it online. We see the country while traveling 70 mph down interstate highways in our automobiles. We experience food in sanitized packages while walking the aisles of climate-controlled supermarkets. Technology has changed our productivity and prosperity. It has changed how we treat illness, how we connect with family, and how we spend our free time.

These changes have started to affect the way we worship. For example, some of us now have our tithes automatically deducted from our bank accounts rather than depositing our donations into the offering plate. Tithing in this way helps us be consistent in our giving and provides churches with a steady income uninterrupted by our travels or illnesses, but it removes one of the few opportunities for communal participation in our worship services. In isolation the practice of tithing via automatic withdrawal may be benign, but what are the implications

49

of living in a world where more and more tasks that once took intentional preparation and action now take place with little effort or thought? This chapter explores the ways that technology increases our power, threatens our knowledge of the world around us, and finally, how it may obscure the church's message of salvation through Christ.

I will follow Shane Hipps in defining technology as, "devices that enhance our God-given abilities." For example, the telephone enhances our ability to communicate by allowing us to talk with people over greater distances than we could with unaided voices. Automobiles allow us to travel farther and faster than we could on our legs. Books allow us to record and remember more information then we could possibly contain in our head. All of these are examples of the ability of different technologies to enhance our natural abilities. The creation of tools and devices (i.e. technology) to accomplish work is not in itself morally good or bad. In Genesis, God instructed Noah to build an ark to preserve his family and the wild animals and livestock. I believe that God fully intends for us to use the mental and physical gifts He has given us to build upon our natural abilities, especially in redemptive ways, such as ark building. However, a couple of chapters later, God is not pleased with the builders of the tower of Babel who were also pursuing a technological project — a project meant not only to extend their physical position (to get higher) but also to indulge their pride and "make a name for themselves" (Gen. 11:4). This was a literal attempt to exalt the individual. Here we have a non-redemptive, inappropriate use of technology.

Thus technology gives us increased power that can be used for redemptive or fallen purposes. Since Americans typically embrace technology for its potential, this chapter will explore the potential for technology to corrupt the message of the church. The goal is not to convince you that technology is evil. It isn't. Instead, I hope to challenge you to think about the subtle impact technology has in our churches.

It may be hard to read this and not think of the Amish and similar Anabaptist groups that quite famously renounce modern technology. Are the Amish right? I believe they are right to think of technology as a significant force in shaping our communities and our spiritual lives. Ultimately, my choices are not the same as the Amish and yours may be different still, but I hope all our choices are informed not by what is cool or the latest thing, but rather by what allows us to participate in and further the redemptive work of our Savior.

Technology Increases Power

We use technology to eliminate, or at least mitigate, conditions that cause human suffering — to provide appropriate shelter, clothing, and food while reducing pain. Over time we have been able to progress from fortifying human beings against the hardships of life to eliminating the hardships entirely. We don't need several heavy blankets to protect against the cold air if we can warm the air to a comfortable temperature. Rather than subsisting on food carefully preserved from the last harvest, we can transport fresh food to any location in the world year-round. This has allowed us to shift from using technology as a means of simple survival to using technology for the less pressing daily inconveniences we all experience.

We have found increasingly clever ways of using technology to make things more convenient. We don't have to haul water from a well or stream anymore; it comes directly to several places in our homes, and we expect it to come at a variety of temperatures we can easily control for different tasks. All of this technological success has led to increased expectations for comfort: Almost no inconvenience is too petty to be addressed by some technological solution. Consequently, we no longer seek the patience and strength to endure hardships; we seek a device that will eliminate them, even if the hardship is changing the channel on our television. Technology used daily for our personal comfort is a hallmark of life in third-millennium America.

Churches have also used technology to increase the comfort of worshipers, from microphones and speakers to amplify the message to pagers that keep parents connected to the nursery. We expect good parking, lighting, and signage in churches. We use screens and handouts to provide a unified translation of Scripture and sermon notes to help us track with the speaker. Thus we have used the power of technology both inside and outside of church to make our worship more comfortable.

Technology gives us the power to largely overcome the obstacle of our differing opinions of what is comfortable. What one person may enjoy may be unsatisfactory to someone else. To account for these individual differences, we created a variety of tools that allow each person to customize their experience. Tired of listening to what everyone else is listening to? The iPod is the latest in a string of popular gadgets that allow you to create a personal soundtrack to your daily activities. This is one of many devices that illustrate our increasing desire for technologies used exclusively by a single individual. While churches still work hard to foster shared communal experiences, it is not uncommon to find churches that allow members to load worship services on those same iPods for personal consumption at the time and place the listener chooses. As mentioned above, another example of this trend is giving parishioners the opportunity to personalize their tithing through online options that allow people to pick the time and frequency of their donations and then automate the entire process, or not, as they choose.

Personalized technology also allows us to distinguish ourselves from our peers. We are given the opportunity to choose the make, model, color, calling plan, ringtone, and wallpaper of our cell phone in order to create a unique cell phone experience. I have a metallic Motorola Razr with an AT&T plan, a University of Nebraska fight song

ringtone (among others), and a picture of the Chicago skyline serves
as my wallpaper, and I will have reconfigured this cell phone identity a
dozen times by the printing of this book. All of these choices help me
to project a certain image, one that I've actively created. Owning an
iPhone or Blackberry would create a different image, as would changing
any of the other listed features.

Giving attendees choices is also important for many
contemporary churches. Not only are we commonly given technological
choices in church such as opening your Bible or looking at the screen
for today's Scripture reading (a choice some expand as they pull up the
reading on a BlackBerry) but we also provide different services, small
groups, classes, ministries, and service teams. People, consciously or
unconsciously, craft for themselves an identity as they choose how to
participate in the church. I choose to attend the Friday couples' small
group, teach a Sunday morning adult Bible fellowship, and usually
attend the 11 o'clock service. This illustrates a central argument of
this chapter. Technology affects us when we directly use technological
devices, but the effects extend beyond the obvious. Our frequent
experiences with technology color our expectations for many areas of
our lives — including those where technology may be absent. These
rules continue to apply when we walk through the church doors.

Does the fact that we have so many options when it comes to
cell phones cause churches to package their small group offerings a
certain way? Deciphering a single or simple cause is not my task here.
Instead, I'm suggesting that we live in a world where we have used
technology to provide us with all kinds of choices and options. When
brushing our teeth, we can choose from an endless variety of toothpastes
and brushes. We assume this is normal, and these assumptions start
to color what we expect from other aspects of life, including spiritual
aspects.

PUTTING GOD IN HIS PLACE

Thus we use technology to create choices that satisfy our unique understanding of comfort and to communicate who we are and what we value. However, all of us may be unaware of how these common uses of technology influence the way we approach the world. We may not consciously reflect on whether it is better to have a self-propelled lawn mower or the strength and discipline to operate a non-gas-powered push lawn mower, but repeatedly choosing path of least resistance leaves us weaker and unprepared for difficult tasks. In the church, too, we can let uncritical assumptions about the value of personal comfort and individual choices color our message. We may teach that Christians must deny themselves but then offer programs catering to every demographic niche in our congregation, reinforcing the opposite cultural message that we should indulge our preferences.

The power afforded us by our mastery of technology has implications beyond those sketched above. We have used technology to change our relationship to time; we increasingly expect things to happen immediately at the touch of a button. We have also become accustomed to high levels of control over our environment and experiences. The fact that technology does provide a great measure of control and compresses the time required for many activities also has profound implications for what we expect out of church and from our relationship with God. Many find the discipline of waiting upon the Lord increasingly difficult when we aren't accustomed to waiting for other types of information. Likewise, the reality that we serve a transcendent and holy God conflicts with our expectation of control.

While concrete, positive proposals await in part two of this book, I conclude here that technology enhances our abilities to communicate, create, work, and travel. This means that it can enhance the redemptive work that we are called to do, but it can also feed our pride and inclination to place ourselves at the center of the universe. The very devices that empower the proclamation of the Gospel also can impede the reception of that message by building in all of us a sense of entitlement to a comfortable life bounded by personal choices in which we expect to exercise a great deal of control over how and when things happen. This is a life at odds with the life of faith taught and modeled by Christ.

Technology May Diminish Knowledge

Technology makes things easier, which is one reason we value it. In most cases using technology requires less force or exertion on our part. Loading clothes in a washing machine is not as much work as scrubbing them on a washboard. Playing a Bach fugue on a CD player takes far less effort than playing it on an organ. Not only does technology save physical labor, but it often reduces the amount of knowledge that we need. Knowledge not needed can easily be lost. Thus, technology can damage our knowledge of daily tasks, the natural world, moral issues, and other people. Each of these realities have implications for the church that must be considered as well.

Technology typically requires less knowledge of the underlying task being done. I don't need to know anything about music to push play on my stereo, and I don't need to know anything about radiation or cooking to make microwaveable popcorn. We can ride airplanes and drive cars without knowing about aerodynamics or combustion engines. In other words, we can get the desired results from our devices without understanding the underlying principles that are producing those results. Indeed we might need to learn how to set the microwave properly not to burn the popcorn (use power setting 1 for 45 seconds), but this knowledge of how to manipulate the settings on the machine tells us nothing about how our food is being prepared. The point here is that if we fall into the pattern of being only interested in the result and neglect learning the reason why things work, we lose an important type of knowledge.

PUTTING GOD IN HIS PLACE

In our churches we also use technology to make things easy, potentially at the expense of knowledge. We reproduce Scripture passages so parishioners don't need to spend time looking up the passage, or know where Isaiah is, or even bring their Bible to church. It is easy to purchase videos of all-star Bible teachers for our adult education (or children's classes) rather than allow members of the local congregation to teach. Lost in this practice is the knowledge and confidence that comes from creating and delivering one's own lessons. Within such an environment, lay leaders may conclude that explaining Scripture is an activity they are not qualified for and could not do.

More significantly, our ability to perform great physical feats with little physical or mental effort can lead us to falsely believe that we can achieve significant spiritual growth with equally little effort. We can also treat Christian rites such as communion and confession as spiritual keys to turn or buttons to push while failing to appreciate the spiritual realities in play or the profound commitment they should call forth in ourselves. Since so little in our world demands sustained attention the fact that true Christian discipleship does require high levels of dedication and sacrifice may be missed.

This warning may seem odd in an "information age" when we have unprecedented resources at our fingertips. Indeed, we can use information technology to acquire new knowledge, but true learning still takes time and effort. Unfortunately, the vast amounts of information available to us may actually discourage deep engagement with ideas. When crafting a sermon, for example, we can copy and paste the illustrations and insights of others in lieu of personal reflection upon a text. When used appropriately, the abundance of information available to us is a true blessing, but like material blessings, it can be mishandled to our detriment.

A second way technology threatens knowledge is by insulating us from the material world. We may chuckle at the child who thinks apples come from a grocery store, but the reality is that very few of us have much knowledge about how the food we eat gets produced. Even commercial farmers rely increasingly on all sorts of machinery and chemicals to provide us with the grains and meats we take for granted. The production and distribution of food is just one example of how technology insulates us from the natural world. This does not mean that we need to abandon all our agricultural technology. I'm grateful not to live under the constant fear of famine, as so many of our ancestors did, and I think we should all be thankful that medical technology that insulates us from some of the dangers that would otherwise threaten us in our fallen world. Nevertheless, the bounty provided us by our technology can obscure the fact that we remain creatures formed from the dust and that we are dependent on God's creation. We become vulnerable to the lie that says we have mastered the natural world and are no longer subject to its rules. Ultimately this lie leads to a degraded, ugly physical environment and impoverished lives.

An additional danger of being insulated from the material world is that we miss out on the wonder and awe produced by encountering God's creation. For Christians this engagement with the natural world is often an invitation to worship. The devices we create, no matter how shiny or slick, rarely produce similar results. A television, despite the colors it brilliantly reproduces, is unlikely to foster a sense of worship, though a quiet walk in the woods frequently does. One possible exception to this is the great works of human art. Such works, unlike our mechanical creations, are usually intended to provide illumination of the created world rather than insulation from it.

At their best, our church practices and programs illuminate the spiritual realities of our world and lead us to worship. This requires constant vigilance, lest our religious practices devolve into empty forms that insulate us from spiritual reality rather than illuminating it. Taking a multiple-choice spiritual gift inventory, for example, may illuminate the mysterious and exciting work of the Spirit in the church, but it can also become a tool that tames God for consumption. Amid all the strategic plans, targeted ministries, and community outreach events, we need to remember that their task is to bring us into relationship with the Holy God who can shake us and transform us, and that all of these processes need to be carried out in a manner that glorifies God.

Success at manipulating the world with technological devices also imperils our moral knowledge. It is easy to see the world as a series of problems that technology either has solved or is working on solving. The fact that not everybody in the world has enough to eat can be seen as a challenge to our agricultural technology to produce and distribute even more food; however, viewing the world this way obscures the moral dimensions of the problem. We are called to discern light from darkness and good from evil, but this is not a task with which our machines can help. Technology can alleviate some of the symptoms of injustice, but it does not address the root cause. The fact remains that we are all sinners. In some cases, technology can be a distraction from considering our moral responsibility to our neighbors. For example, we may focus exclusively on how we can improve food production rather than curtail our often gluttonous consumption. Consideration of the moral status of an activity is another type of knowledge frequently obscured by the hype of "new and improved" technological solutions.

Likewise, churches can easily see new programs and procedures as solutions to our problems. Perhaps these will be truly helpful, but we also need to evaluate our spiritual health. At times only repentance and spiritual renewal will address what is truly ailing us. There is a need for all to be reminded that we cannot invent a solution for every problem; in fact, the only solution for our greatest problem is the gift of the incarnation.

Finally, technology can also reduce our knowledge of other people. Technology gives us incredible opportunities to connect with people all over the world. Social networking sites on the internet allow us to stay connected with the scores of people we meet throughout our lives, while other applications allow us to talk to people around the world while watching them on a live video feed, all for very little cost. These services provide real value in this age when we so freely move around the globe. They also provide great tools for the church to stay connected to missionaries and other Christians who are serving the Lord in remote places — helping us focus our prayers and provide tangible encouragement.

This new power to extend fellowship can also contribute to a degradation of community if we forget that knowing another person is always limited when mediated through a screen and digital voice connection. There is a deeper knowledge that comes from spending time physically with others, seeing their context, sharing a meal, giving a hug, or even just spending time silently in the same place. A special danger with the way we use this technology is that the vast amount of people we can now talk to or chat with makes it increasingly tempting to value relationships for the way they benefit us. When we need to talk about sports we call Taylor; relationships, Pat; and Chris is our go-to person on home repairs. This way of approaching relationships mirrors the way we use different machines and can cheapen our experience of community.

Paradoxically, technology opens up previously unfathomed amounts of information, but in several important ways it can contribute to a culture in which there are many words but little knowledge. By making things happen at the flip of a switch, we don't have much incentive to understand the complexity of our world. By insulating ourselves from the natural world, we can lose touch with an important part of God's revelation to us. When constantly told that technology can solve our problems, we risk forgetting that the evil that resulted from the Fall can never be engineered out of the universe by human action.

Lastly, we can stay in contact with many people around the globe but can be tempted to think that this replaces being physically present with our brothers and sisters in community.

Technology as a Rival to the Gospel

The Gospel we proclaim is that a fallen humanity separated from God can find reconciliation through faith in the atoning death and resurrection of Christ. This is the foundational message of the church. Technology implicitly diagnoses humanity's problems differently. The hype that surrounds each new advance, no matter how trivial, subtly or openly proclaims that our chief problems are discomfort, a lack of control, and boredom. We are told that new drugs will alleviate our medical conditions, that a new car will keep our family safe from car accidents, and that a new HD television will dazzle us with movies and sports like we've never seen before. But if none of this satisfies — and it never does completely satisfy — we are asked to wait for the next new thing. We have grown accustomed to thinking that the new is always improved over the old and that given time, progress is inevitable. Accepting these terms is a problem for Christians who seek to use technology redemptively to promote the Gospel.

First, the technological paradigm diminishes our felt need for the Gospel by obscuring personal responsibility. No one is asked to repent or is held accountable for the injustice in the world. The technological paradigm implies that given the proper tools, we can remove from our experience everything that troubles us and live a life of pure pleasure. Even crime can be largely removed, so we are led to believe, with more security cameras, improved forensic technology, and better psychological drugs to cure the mentally unstable who commit crimes. When we are assured that technology is responsible for solving the problems in the world, we are also given little motivation to love our neighbors. Indeed, many devices are designed to allow us to have as little contact with our neighbors as possible. Public institutions such as libraries and theaters are being supplanted by machines that give you access to similar services in your own home. Even the street, which was once the archetype of public space where Christ encountered tax collectors and beggars, has been transformed into a largely private and anonymous space as we speed by in our automobiles. Thus technology obscures the fact that, according to the Gospel, we are all sinners, and are responsible for that sin, and that we are all called upon to love our neighbors.

Our promised technological salvation ultimately erodes human dignity as well. What separates humanity from the lower forms of life is our mental capacities, the ability to ask big questions about God, goodness, and beauty, to understand and overcome complex problems. Our technology grows out of these abilities, but when used to create a life of easy, unreflective pleasure it ultimately debases our noblest characteristics. There is little that is noble about a life spent channel surfing on a couch eating Cheetos. Nor is there much that is inspiring in the commonly held view that we are the sum of our genetic parts. We are not simply machines whose difficulties can be removed by rewiring or reprogramming. By using technology to address immediate desires, we lose sight of our cosmic position as God's stewards over all creation, only slightly lower than the angels. We forget that we are called to do battle against the forces of evil and that there is more reward for overcoming challenges than avoiding them. Our world becomes thin and trivial when driven by a quest for personal amusement.

Additionally, the power and control offered by our technological gadgets can provide a false sense of security that obscures our dependence upon God. For example, the shock and awe we can inspire with the destructive power of our modern military machines can allow us to assume victory on the battlefield rather than humbly pray for it. But Isaiah's reminder remains true: It is not technological supremacy that wins battles, or keeps us healthy, or provides food, but the hand of the Lord (Isa. 31:1). For all our pretensions, we remain like the grass of the field that sprouts and vanishes quickly. As Christians we affirm that living in submission to God results in the abundant life, and this view contrasts directly with the promise of many of our devices to give us autonomy and control over our slice of the world.

Therefore, a culture dominated by questions of comfort, control, and diversion leaves us with a flat, sinless world where we act as a multitude of small deities creating our own personalized universes.

In the church we must guard against unwittingly reinforcing this message by accepting its terms. We need to reiterate that the purpose of our life is not ease and endless diversion, but to bring glory to God. We need to reflect on Paul's reminder that suffering can build character and teach more about following our suffering Savior. When many fall into unconsciously praying as though God serves them and not the other way around, we need a church that constantly reminds us who is really in control. Finally, we need teaching that affirms the value of work and direct engagement with God's creation as a more satisfying and uplifting antidote to the boredom that persists despite all the devices designed to entertain us. All of this follows and builds upon the understanding that ultimately we are sinners saved by grace.

Chapter 4

Entertainment

By Mark Coddington

When the topic of cultural influences on Christianity comes up, there are few things Christians love criticizing more than entertainment media. We rail with impunity against Hollywood, cable TV, trashy magazines, the internet and Top 40 radio. Christian publications have addressed the effect of entertainment media, and specifically visual media, on society, the church, the family and the individual at considerable length. I, too, see troubling consequences of our culture's media binge in recent decades, but I believe many of those consequences are coming through a much more subtle — and more insidious — means than we typically see at first glance.

The vast majority of what has caught Christians' eye in visual media has been the content of the media, not its form. Myriad Christian websites and publications keep precise counts of foul language and document in detail sexual and violent content in television shows and movies. This can be a productive exercise and a useful tool for Christians to discern appropriate content in media. For example, some forms of content, such as pornography, are in themselves demeaning and degrading and must be avoided regardless of what form or context they come in. But just as often, content functions as a red herring to distract Christians from the deeper effects of the form of the medium itself.

A typical PG- and R-rated movie might bear critical differences in their content, both in the amount of offensive material and, more importantly, in the philosophies they espouse. But in many cases, those differences pale in comparison with the fact that both are films rather than, say, books. All films, no matter how disparate their content, carry with them a set of assumptions that, consumed on a large scale, play a significant role in informing our lives — values like immediacy, immersive passivity, and the importance of constant stimulation. These influences are often much less immediately apparent than the effects of content, but they are, in the end, at least as critical in shaping our collective mindset. Whether or not one agrees with Marshall McLuhan's famous assertion that the medium is the message, it is clear that the medium we use to communicate indelibly shapes what is communicated.

I offer this critique not as someone who stands outside our media landscape, but instead as someone who, for better or worse, is rather firmly entrenched in it. As a newspaper reporter, exposure to a continual flood of media is an essential part of my working world. Media consumption isn't simply an employment requirement to me, though: I enjoy movies, blogs, radio and podcasts, and relentlessly seek out the best of those forms. But while I'm certainly not opposed to our culture's proliferation of media, I believe it is well worth our time to find out what message that media is communicating and how it affects our churches and lives of faith. Let's start with a picture of what we're facing.

Few institutions in modern America are as stuffed with stimulation as the average evangelical church. Of course, there's no such thing as a perfectly representative evangelical church, but if you walk into almost any evangelical church today, you're bound to encounter at least a few elements, if not more, from the following illustration. A couple visiting an evangelical church's Sunday service walks into an unrelenting barrage of images that divert, distract, and entertain. Once they make it to the sanctuary, they grab a plush seat among hundreds on a downward-sloping floor modeled after a movie theater. They're met with bouncy piano renditions of popular worship choruses as other visitors settle in around them. The two giant screens at the front of the sanctuary rotate through a series of slides advertising the church's upcoming events, each illustrated with a soft-focus photo of a laughing couple, pensive teen, or smiling child.

The service begins with a perky worship leader, sporting a hands-free, ear-mounted microphone, who urges our visitors to stand and clap along to a jangling beat. Lyrics of the song are displayed on the screens with backgrounds of peaceful nature scenes — a gently flowing waterfall, a mountain sunset, a horse galloping through a meadow. After a few minutes, the worship team strides off the stage, and the house lights dim as they are replaced by a drama team performing a short skit in a living room set quickly set up by stagehands. A pastor appears on stage to give announcements and introduces a video promoting next month's women's conference taking place nearby. The video features dozens of shots of speakers, worship bands, women praying, women cheering, women with their hands in the air, all edited together into two minutes of quick cuts, set to an upbeat rock tune.

After another set of worship marked by dim lighting and an emotional performance by the worship leader, the pastor jogs on stage, his face beamed onto the screens that flank him. He begins his message with a long, humorous personal story, then peppers his talk with jokes and anecdotes. The Bible verses he references are displayed on the screens, along with each point of a neat outline to his sermon. He illustrates his final point with a two-minute clip from the movie "Gladiator," which replaces his visage on the screens as the sanctuary is darkened. Finally, he builds to a rousing conclusion, utters a brief prayer, and then dismisses the congregation as the house lights brighten again. Our visitors emerge from their seats speechless, a little dazed, and slowly wander toward the exits.

PUTTING GOD IN HIS PLACE

Your church's weekly service probably isn't the picture I've just described, but at least a few elements were likely familiar to you. The service also wasn't meant to entertain — in fact, it was probably intended to encourage and evangelize — but thanks to some cultural realities that we'll look at below, what resulted was an hourlong cavalcade of entertainment.

From Discourse to Distraction

Of course, church in America wasn't always this way. Services in the 18th-century New England churches in which evangelicalism was born took place in nondescript meeting houses, with austere exteriors, wooden benches, and nothing adorning the walls except possibly a simple cross. Worship was done without instruments, and sermons in many churches would run for an hour or two. Rarely were they punctuated with anecdotes or flashy displays of emotion. Contemporary accounts of the great 18th-century preacher Jonathan Edwards' famous sermon "Sinners in the Hands of an Angry God" note that the message, which is known for its vivid picture of God's impending wrath, was delivered in little more than a monotone and read from a manuscript with eyes barely leaving the page. Yet the sermon left its listeners rapt with attention and, ultimately, overcome with tears.

To be sure, American churches in centuries past had something to stimulate their congregants, too; one need only look as far as the breathtaking stained glass of St. Patrick's Cathedral or imagine the booming voice of Edwards' contemporary, George Whitefield, to demonstrate that. But the stimulation of our churches today is unprecedented in its rapidity. Whereas a single sweeping mural of a biblical scene might continue to be mined for insight for years, the modern worship service is calculated to change every week, minute, or even every few seconds. And where the church has historically used its own vocabulary of artistic and oratorical styles, today's church borrows heavily from the language of America's culture of celebrity and entertainment to inform its understanding of what church should look, sound, and feel like. Our spiritual ancestors would likely recoil in confusion and horror if they were among the visitors to the service described previously, and it wouldn't just be a result of the leaps we've taken in technology since their time. Along with those advances — and in large part because of them — we've evolved into a church that, however subconsciously, values entertainment and stimulation right alongside such biblical virtues as service, community, and even obedience.

How did we get here? More than anything else, our addiction to amusement can be traced back to one cultural shift — from a primarily verbal culture to a visual one. The effects of this sea change have been documented by many scholars far more capably than I could, most notably by Neil Postman in his classic 1986 work *"Amusing Ourselves to Death: Public Discourse in the Age of Show Business,"* so I will only give a cursory summary of its ramifications. Until the early 20th century, American culture was dominated by the written word. Newspapers, telegraphs, and letters were the primary means of spreading information and documenting events. Most public oratory was literary in nature, deftly building a complex set of arguments to reach a logical conclusion. Its vocabulary, though commonly understood during its time, was so elevated compared with today's that many modern readers find it nearly incomprehensible. Elements of showmanship were prominent in forms of discourse, including religious speech: Benjamin Franklin once remarked of Whitefield's stump sermons that "every accent, every emphasis, every modulation of voice, was so perfectly well turn'd and well plac'd, that, without being interested in the subject, one could not help being pleas'd with the discourse." But even Whitefield's sermons could go on for hours, with even common people absorbing and understanding his every rhetorical flourish.

In the 1950s, the television reached most American homes and brought to fruition what began with the telegraph — a new focus on immediacy and suspicion of complexity. Television was not America's first visual mass medium: The photograph arrived about a century earlier. Both media shared an emphasis on visceral impact to convey their messages, for there is no place for context in a visual image. By themselves, a photograph or video clip brought its viewers no intellectual information; that had to be supplied through accompanying words or by the viewer herself. Since true intellectual interaction in such an encounter was difficult, the visual images reached the viewers' emotions first. Take, for example, the famous (and infamously staged) 1944 Joe Rosenthal photograph "Raising the Flag on Iwo Jima," depicting five U.S. Marines and one Navy corpsman raising the American flag on the island of Iwo Jima. The photo itself told Americans nothing about why the soldiers were raising the flag, how they got there or what the act or surrounding battle meant within the United States' war against Japan. It was utterly unhelpful in informing Americans about what was going on in the war. But that was not its intended purpose — it was intended to stir up feelings of pride, patriotism, triumph, and support for the U.S. military effort. All were emotional appeals, and all were accomplished perfectly.

But while television shared photography's visceral impact and inability to contextualize information, it also added a time-sensitivity that was new to American culture. Television programming was fleeting, with one scene quickly being replaced by another, only to vanish into dim memory. The transience of television was especially evident in news coverage, where stories had to be condensed into small enough nuggets to be understood without serious thought and where striking video footage began to take precedence over more pressing, but drier, issues. The difference can be seen quite simply in looking at the change in presidential campaign discourse: The famous Lincoln-Douglas debates of the 1850s included addresses that were several hours long, while the average sound bite from the 2004 presidential campaign was 7.73 seconds. Interestingly, the Indiana University researchers who calculated that total found that the length of "image bites," in which candidates are seen but not heard on television, increased as the more substantive sound bites shrank.

Those changes had a profound effect on Americans' ability to understand rational discourse and their desire to seek it out. On television, everything became entertainment. Today's news is a continual stream of shouting pundits, breathless reports, and shocking videos with almost nothing in common but their ability to suck us in. Educational television replaces drills and facts with puppets, jingles, and loosely connected stories. Reality television has turned even the most mundane rituals of everyday life into a commodity to be either mocked or fawned over, but ultimately in either case to entertain. With all those widely disparate areas of experience jammed into one common mold whose primary purpose is to draw our attention, it's easy to see how entertainment became an overarching purpose in our lives, well beyond television. Indeed, television has taught us to focus on one primal desire — does it grab my attention? — and if the answer is no, to move on to the next stimulus until we're satisfactorily amused.

Consequences for the Church

Not surprisingly, the written word falls pretty low on the priority list within that mindset. And when the written word is neglected, our ability to understand it — to comprehend its nuances, to see its arguments through, to appreciate its beauty — fades as well. This gaping hole in understanding is particularly troubling for Christians, for it is largely through the written word that God — the Word Himself —

has revealed His character. God's fullest revelation of Himself, the very "image of the invisible God" (Col. 1:15), was the Incarnation of His Son, the Word become flesh. Two thousand years later, we encounter that living Word through God's written Word. God has used nonverbal means to make Himself known to us, from miracles to the presence of the Holy Spirit. But what has been preserved for us as the medium in which God has chosen to reveal His plan of salvation is not a series of pictures or a sharp-looking video, but hundreds of thousands of words passed down through the ages with a treasure trove of metaphors, arguments, narratives, and subtleties waiting to be uncovered. The Old Testament even includes an ode to the power of the Word in Psalm 119, which simultaneously celebrates the written Law of God and, through its acrostic format, the very alphabet that allowed it to be written and read. Today, as throughout the time Scripture was being written, that written Word of God comes to us primarily through two means: personal study and public proclamation and teaching. Our society's devaluation of and disinterest in the written word in favor of more entertaining visual media has damaged our ability to receive and understand the Word in both forms.

First, we have lost a sense of the eternality of the Word. In a culture in which an internet-driven 24-hour news cycle chews up stories and moves on before they can even be properly understood, it is difficult for many of us to provide a context for works that have been written 200 years ago, let alone 2,000. Likewise, visual culture's focus on newness and the "here and now" may lead us to wonder whether it would be possible for any work of art or literature to last forever, not to mention whether we would find that desirable. Our churches are not helping, either. When Scripture passages referred to in sermons are placed on giant screens as part of a PowerPoint presentation, they are wiped away just as quickly as nursery announcements that came before them, giving the impression that the two are equally temporal. Soon, the attribute of eternality gets replaced by pejoratives like "old" or "antiquated" and the Word can become, in our eyes, irrelevant.

With verbal culture no longer prominent, our intellectual capacity has steadily narrowed. Even basic tasks of biblical comprehension have become a chore, and therefore something to be avoided. Why try to understand the Apostle Paul's purpose in writing Philippians when we can just remember Philippians 4:13 and try to internalize the idea that "I can do all things through Christ who strengthens me"? Our reflections on our faith are similarly bite-sized, as evidenced by the popularity of devotionals that package an entire life of Christian reflection into easily digestible daily "thoughts" with little connection to each other or any broader narrative of faith. And many pastors have succumbed to the reduced attention spans of their parishioners, trading the careful reasoning and hard-won insights of their predecessors for shallow, clichéd messages that can be easily portrayed on a PowerPoint presentation, preferably with alliterative points. A cycle is created: Christians' verbal and rational comprehension slowly atrophy, leading their teachers to challenge them less, which in turn furthers their regression.

This narrowing of cerebral interest has exacerbated an issue particularly prevalent in Protestant America for hundreds of years — anti-intellectualism, or the active animosity toward those with more intellectual tendencies than us. Now more than ever, Americans prefer straight talk from our political and spiritual leaders, eyeing complexity and nuance with suspicion. We're proud of being common people, "just folks" — and anyone who doesn't share our sensibilities is deemed out of touch or elitist. In church, this leads to the assumption that if a parishioner doesn't understand a sermon, Sunday school lesson or worship song, it must be the church's fault. If a pastor's sermons or Bible studies are "too deep," that too often causes us not to push deeper in our own faith, but to throw up our hands and either complain or go elsewhere.

PUTTING GOD IN HIS PLACE

When everything is measured based on its entertainment value, we, of course, enjoy the position of the ultimate arbiter. Even if a book, event, or idea comes to us with authority attached, the power is ours to affix the "boring" tag and dismiss it. This induces a seismic shift in the center of worship. Instead of being a place where we check our desires and gripes at the door to glorify and serve the God who orders the universe, church becomes just another place for us to be entertained. It's not unlike going to a movie: We sit in our seats, absorb what's put in front of us, silently evaluate the performance and make a value judgment. When it's all over, the question we ask each other is not "Did it glorify God?" but "Did you like it?"

Churches play into this approach, seeing their services and programs as a way to keep members' attention. As a response to their congregations' entertain-me mindsets, this is not necessarily a bad thing — it's tough to argue in favor of monotonous preaching and un-engaging lessons. But churches wade into dangerous waters when they start to believe entertainment value has a place in programming discussions alongside worship, obedience, and God's glory. Simply put, the truth and the Word cannot be sacrificed to make church more palatable.

One result of that approach has been the crossover of what Postman calls the "Now . . . This" phenomenon from television to church. The phrase, according to Postman, "is commonly used on radio and television newscasts to indicate that what one has just heard or seen has no relevance to what one is about to hear or see, or possibly to anything one is ever likely to hear or see." It's an acknowledgement that many elements of our rapid-fire visual culture have absolutely no rational order or logical connection with each other — they've all been wiped out by easy replacement of one image with another. With order thus disintegrated from much of the rest of our culture, we've come to expect the same from the church, and it has responded. The result is a church service that feels more like an incoherent jumble of unrelated events than a cohesive time of worship, thanksgiving, instruction, and community. The hypothetical church of the beginning of this chapter is a good example: Songs are followed by a skit, then a video and a sermon, with little, if any, indication of a relationship between them. The central purpose that shines through in such a service is the importance of each individual segment's entertainment value.

The Crossover of Celebrity

The central figure among that parade of images — besides, of course, the churchgoer, to whom all this is catered — is the pastor. Everything about his presence communicates his importance. His place alone at the center of the stage stands in contrast to the American Puritans, who placed their pulpits near the side of their meeting halls so as to preserve the centrality of the cross. Coupled with his face's constant appearance on the screens around him, the message is clear: This man is someone important, someone to follow.

The celebrity status being subtly reinforced in this scenario is part of a larger, society-wide fixation on celebrities fueled by the glut of celebrity images pushed throughout the visual media — film, television, magazine photography. With an ever-larger array of information reaching us and a simultaneously flatlining amount of substantial discourse, much of that widening gap is being spent trying to sate our hunger for celebrities to obsess over. Surely, celebrity is not a new phenomenon, but the nature of American celebrity since the early 1900s is unlike anything seen before. In past centuries, people achieved celebrity through their achievements, whether they won battles, wrote literature, or led an empire. But only recently has the culture of celebrity taken root so deeply that people can become the object of our attention and adoration for no reason other than that we are fed information about them and told that we should care. They are, as the saying goes, "famous for being famous." This is no doubt fueled by the explosion of visual media over the past half-century, which has extended the breadth and depth of fame arguably beyond any other culture in history. And our appetite has kept pace with it.

The church has borrowed that language of celebrity, using cues established by Hollywood and Madison Avenue to trigger our fixation on certain individuals. Some of those codes are obvious — pastors with their own television shows or with their faces gracing the covers of bestselling self-help books — but others operate far more subtly. Take, for example, that ear-mounted microphone the pastor and worship leader in our example are wearing. It's perfectly practical, allowing speakers and singers use of both hands while avoiding the awkwardness of a lapel mic. But its presence connotes celebrity and importance, whether intended or not. It was popularized during the 1990s by megastar musicians such as Garth Brooks and Britney Spears, and that level of celebrity is the subconscious association that it often carries when worn, especially by someone who's energetically crisscrossing the stage like a rock star might.

And with those connotations comes the baggage of celebrity. It comes in the passive voyeurism that's encouraged by the movie theater-style seating centered on the stage, the attitude that brings a parishioner to church to watch someone they're in awe of, rather than to participate. It comes in the cult of personality that can lead congregations to follow a charismatic leader, blind to his faults, into heresy. And it comes in the unquestioning trust that people can develop for Christian leaders with whom they've never actually communicated, based largely on their charisma on television or popularity in book sales.

It might appear that the unwitting encouragement of celebrity is limited to megachurches, but the effects of celebrity culture have spread far beyond that setting. Because of that culture's omnipresence, many small-church pastors have begun to take their cues, often consciously, from their celebrity counterparts. This creates a simulacrum effect in which smaller churches emulate larger churches' techniques, hoping to tap into their success. In this area, at least, the megachurch has gone Main Street.

Of course, churches have always used visual cues to draw distinctions between clergy and laity, whether through collars, stoles, or robes. But this visual language of celebrity culture is one that comes from outside the church, one that has been absorbed by American Christianity from the culture around it. The church is not obligated to draw on an external cultural language to communicate the authority of clergy; it can draw on its deep well of symbols.

The Coarsening of Conversation

One of the offshoots of the visual revolution that has picked up steam in the past decade or two is television news' transformation of complex, weighty political and cultural issues into shouting matches pitting opposing pundits against each other. These issues may have countless facets or gray areas or nuances, but on television, they are turned into black-and-white issues featuring representatives of two polar-opposite positions. And the objective is not understanding, but determining a winner or loser, for the pleasure of the audience: It's news as a game show. (ESPN's "Around the Horn" has taken this concept literally, turning its shout-fest with sports columnists into a contest in which the host gives points and determines a winner based on his approval of their arguments.) This phenomenon has been popularly and rightly maligned in recent years, but that criticism does not negate its influence on us.

Not surprisingly, it has helped lead us to see things in black-and-white and ultimately antagonistic terms everywhere we look, including in church. Those who don't agree with us about the style of worship music, the qualifications of the pastoral candidate, or the color of the nursery carpet are not to be understood and compromised with; they are to be opposed and defeated. Those in the church have always fought among themselves, but the form of that fighting has increasingly been characterized by shout-downs and sound bites. It's not hard to see the division that results.

Our talking-head culture has also led us to attach personalities with ideas to the point that the ideas themselves often fade into the background. What matters to us is not so much the idea being presented (or shouted); it's the label next to the name of the person who's presenting it. We rarely judge ideas on their own merit, and we consider no one unbiased or fair in their thought — the announcers calling the game are always against our team, and the opposing political party is always out to harm the country. This can be a dangerous suspicion when transferred to church settings, where it might exacerbate our inclination to dismiss perfectly wise advice from people we don't like or assume that virtually everyone (except ourselves, of course) has some sort of malicious angle on a church discussion.

Throughout their many manifestations, these assumptions attached to entertainment media have imprinted the church with their distaste for substance and preoccupation with diversion. Perhaps most troubling, they run deeper than the life of the church, into our relationship with God Himself. Visual media has helped fill every inch of our lives with noise. Very little of it has any real meaning, but it is always there — constantly buzzing, squawking, clamoring for our attention. Silence feels intimidating, overwhelming, suffocating, so we fill it with something — anything, really. When we commune with God, the phenomenon is no different: We can't stand silence, especially silence that doesn't immediately produce a revelation, so we fill the space with our near-sighted and confused rambling. Instead, we might do well to learn from the Lord's appearance to the prophet Elijah. We are surrounded with the insipid blaring of television, but the Lord is not in it. Then we see the spectacle and pretended weightiness of film, but the Lord is not in it. Then comes the limitless smorgasbord of the internet, but the Lord is not that, either. We must clear out room amid the din for the Word of the Lord, lest that still, small voice float past us altogether.

Part II

Moving Forward

Introduction

Over the course of the last chapters, we've gone through the sometimes painful process of demonstrating how four great reality-shaping aspects of our culture show little regard for whatever boundaries we might suppose to exist between sacred and secular. The ideological byproducts of technology, democracy, entertainment, and the marketplace shape the church in ways we easily notice, and more troublingly, in ways we often miss. Each of the four aspects of our culture we explored affirms and lends itself to the exaltation of the individual.

Individuals encounter the marketplace and unintentionally bring its principles with them to worship. Churches, in turn, obscure the Gospel and elevate the individual by uncritically adopting these marketplace maxims. The American cultural dogma of "one person, one vote" promotes the individual to the role of prime actor on life's stage. In the church, nurturing these selfish impulses undermines the authority of Scripture, challenges the unity of Christ's body, and makes the Gospel and church participation about personal fulfillment. Technology offers us a rival Gospel that promises the power to gratify our cravings for comfort, control, and diversion without requiring much knowledge of our world. The preeminence of our visual media has fueled an addiction to amusement that devalues the Word and establishes our desire to be entertained as a focal point of our involvement in church.

PUTTING GOD IN HIS PLACE

When we are inclined to abandon hope, Matthew 16 reminds us that Christ promised He would build His church. No matter how powerful forces aligned against it may seem, the power of Christ to nurture and protect His bride is infinitely greater. We are not the first generation of believers to be confronted with a fallen culture. Throughout history, Christ has equipped the church to face the challenges of their respective eras.

Our faith in Christ's faithfulness moves us to offer the church these ideas for bringing Kingdom thinking to bear on the cultural realities in third-millennium America.

All the suggestions in this chapter are offered under the umbrella of a single constructive principle, and best articulated by John the Baptist: "He must increase, but I must decrease" (John 3:30). If the common problem fostered by the four cultural realities we've considered is the exaltation of the individual, then the appropriate response is the exaltation of God over ourselves. Although we recognize this is the overarching purpose of the church throughout history, we believe it still needs to be asserted because there are subtle forces at work that undermine it.

In what follows we offer four constructive proposals along with some practical suggestions for how we might respond to the cultural forces that exaggerate the position of the individual. As you read, you'll notice that our suggestions aren't entirely new. We've tried to reapply classic Christian principles to the cultural challenges confronting the church in third-millennium America.

Underneath the constructive principle stated earlier, we offer the following four proposals:

1. Let the Gospel speak
2. Interpret actively and faithfully
3. Embrace substance
4. Strive for simplicity

Moving Forward

With each proposal, we'll offer a rationale, an explanation of how the proposal addresses the challenges discussed in the preceding chapters, and a series of suggested practices as a starting point for taking action.

Chapter 5

Let the Gospel Speak

By Aron Utecht

What do we mean by "Let the Gospel speak?" An answer actually begs a more fundamental question: "What is the Gospel?" The Greek word euangelion is the word we translate as Gospel. The most basic definition is good news, by which we mean generally God's plan of salvation for the forgiveness of human sin. Here's a brief sketch of some of the specifics I believe the term Gospel encompasses.

At its most basic level, it is good news that we, as humans who are trapped in our own sin and unable to free ourselves, can be reconciled to God through Jesus' payment on our behalf on the cross. This is the essence of the Gospel, yet the New Testament also provides other components that are essential for understanding the term. Jesus speaks about taking up our cross and following Him (Matt. 16:24) and expecting persecution (Matt. 5:10-11; John 16:33). Peter and Paul both speak of a command to repent (Acts 2:38; 17:30), indicating the Gospel is an offer of a gracious gift, but also a command that must be obeyed (2 Thess. 1:8; 1 Pet. 4:17). Peter and Paul also speak of suffering for the cause of the Gospel (1 Thess. 3:4; 1 Pet. 4:12). Jesus Himself was perfected through suffering; we who follow Him should expect no less (Heb. 2:10). And a dominant theme of Revelation is an exhortation to perseverance despite the inevitable suffering for the name of Christ (Rev. 2:10-11). The New Testament writers emphasize the resurrection of Jesus as vindication as God's Messiah (Rom. 1:4). His coming to judge all of humanity and vindicate the faithful at some future point is a frightening prospect — so much so, that to leave that detail out borders on misleading. Salvation can't be earned, but our faith in Jesus needs to connect with the reality that we'll stand before Him someday to answer for all we've done.

The Gospel announces that in the person of Jesus, the Kingdom — the rule and reign of God — has broken in on human history. As such, evil's days are numbered. At an hour already appointed but not revealed to us, all suffering and death will be put away. All those who have persecuted God's saints of every age will be brought to justice, and Satan himself will be punished for his rebellion. All those who have chosen faithfulness over accommodation will be vindicated.

This is the Gospel. And many a faithful witness has faced down lions, and surrendered themselves to prison, torture, or flames to remain true to it. We owe it to them and ourselves to take care not to neglect any aspect.

Paul says in Romans 1:16 that the Gospel "is the power of God for the salvation of everyone who believes." Honestly, as one who is called to preach, what do I really think I can contribute to the power of God? Wouldn't I do better to just get out of the way and let God speak for Himself? Or am I charged with contextualizing an ancient message for a (post)modern audience? Perhaps the path of wisdom involves some of both. But we would advocate more of the former, and less of the latter. Here's briefly how this proposal relates to the cultural assumptions we've outlined.

How This Proposal Addresses Those Concerns Raised in Earlier Chapters

Our cultural assumptions from the marketplace tell us that the value of any message is contingent on its marketability. But the value of the Gospel is found in its truthfulness. It is true not because it works better than other religious brands, but because God has revealed it and it corresponds to reality. It is not a commodity to be bought, sold or traded. We have no corner on it. We cannot brand it or associate it with other images or concepts that might help it connect with people. Unlike toothpaste, jeans, cars, or beer, the Gospel does not need us to sell it. Those products are inanimate and will not sell themselves. The Gospel has power. The Holy Spirit is actively working and drawing people. God has invited us to partner with Him. But we need to keep straight who's leading the dance. The Gospel has stood for two millennia. We don't need to finesse it, nuance it, or shelter people from certain aspects to make it more appealing.

If living in a democracy elevates the individual, the Gospel is the perfect antidote. Democratic assumptions tell us that we are the source of authority, that we are in the position of influence, and that we (as the collective) are king. By contrast, the Gospel radically disabuses us of the notion that we are any source of authority, that we ought to have any position of influence in the realm of creation, and that we are king. It is true that God sending His Son to die on our behalf is ennobling. Yet the Gospel places humans in the place of need, not power. It makes us humbly dependent on our Creator, whereas democracy only nurtures a sense of independence.

The modern myth of technology is that it can heal all ills. We hope to alleviate suffering, solve food and fuel shortages, eliminate disease, and make life and labor more efficient, comfortable, and convenient. Those goals seem worthy, but they don't get to our real problem: sin. It is a spiritual problem at its root, and it must have a spiritual solution. That answer is the Gospel of redemption in Jesus. In trying to enhance our preaching of the Gospel with technological accoutrements we risk sending an unspoken message that the Gospel really isn't sufficient on its own.

PUTTING GOD IN HIS PLACE

We are a culture obsessed with diversion. Blaise Pascal observes regarding our need to be entertained:

The only thing that consoles us for our miseries is diversion, and yet this is the greatest of our miseries. For it is this which principally hinders us from reflecting upon ourselves, and which makes us insensibly ruin ourselves. Without this we should be in a state of weariness, and this weariness would spur us on to seek a more solid means of escaping from it. But diversion amuses us, and leads us, gradually and without ever adverting to it, to death.

Wrapping the Gospel in entertainment media only muddles the message and numbs our own sensitivity to our need for it. We don't preach the Gospel because it is interesting; we preach it because it is true.

Constructive Practices

Here are a few practical suggestions with some relevant explanation. My hope is to help the church counter our cultural influences and allow God's Word and the Gospel to speak for itself.

• Read and teach all of Scripture. There is a natural temptation to teach and preach the parts of Scripture that are easier for people to take. It is no fun to stand on stage in front of people and call out sin or preach on subjects you know will divide people. However unpopular we might feel, teaching through a book of the Bible sends a very strong unspoken message: God has spoken, and this gathering of His people doesn't want to miss anything. That is an unmistakable way to exalt God.

• Teach to the text and not the audience. One of the great strengths of evangelical Christianity is that it is very action-oriented. No Bible lesson or sermon is complete until some sort of specific action(s) have been prescribed from the passage at hand. This, however, unintentionally puts the focus on the audience, instead of God. One way to exalt God and take the focus off of us, His creatures, is to emphasize what we commonly call "application" less. Of course, the Bible is inherently applicable because it is first and foremost the revelation of God's character and His plan. Every word of Scripture is applicable precisely because it is the truest definition of reality — God Himself. Understanding God, the ultimate source for reality, in turn, defines our own reality; therefore, the first level of application is found in aligning our thinking and conduct with the reality of God's character and plan. I contend that the greatest goal we could achieve in our preaching and teaching is to take people into the world of the biblical text in all its wonder, intricacies, and artistic beauty. It is in that world that God primarily reveals Himself today, and it is in that world where we should direct our congregations to discover Him, in whom we live and move and have our being. We should first and foremost bring people into the story of God and allow them to get lost in that world. Our natural desire is to fast-forward through this more difficult, abstract step and teach the Bible in ways that will give others a more concrete takeaway that they can apply immediately through action. As we've shown, though, much of our culture is already reinforcing the notion that everything revolves around us. The unintended message in always having some kind of individually applied, action-oriented application is that the Bible is really about us. Most of Scripture, though, does not concern itself with us. The vast majority of God's Word is narrative, or some other genre that gives us a window into the character and nature of God, but doesn't give us any specific directives. Let the messages of those passages stand on their own. I am not at all saying here that pastors and teachers should not work to apply the Bible or give people practical tips for Christian living. I am saying that perhaps that healthy desire is a bit out of balance. Overemphasizing application does not necessarily align us to God's reality, but could unwittingly foster a Christianity that encourages us only to tweak a few behaviors.

One example: For a recent adult Sunday school series at our church, I wrote a study that was a theological survey of Acts. As a genre, Acts is a theological narrative. Luke included what he did to tell us certain truths about God's character and His work in salvation history. So I tried to pick some of the most important passages that advanced Luke's theological message. Technically speaking, narrative can't be directly applied to individual situations because it doesn't give us any instruction. It doesn't tell us to do anything. But there were still many implications discussed as we closed the lessons. Still, the bulk of the time and energy was spent on hearing the inspired author's message. Most lessons succeeded in stirring people's engagement with the Scripture and reflection on how and why God works the way He does. Then we turned to some principles that might carry over into contemporary life.

• Engage the Scriptures directly in a corporate setting. More time simply reading Scripture together can also help to let God speak for Himself. Most church services have been honed to an hour, or hour and fifteen minutes. In that kind of environment where time is such a commodity, what we stop and give our attention to communicates our values. Take time to read entire portions of Scripture, without feeling the rush to summarize and "get to the point" — perhaps one whole Psalm, or a passage that complements the passage for the message. Just God's Word read, to His people, with no human explanation can help exalt God and give His creatures a proper perspective. Isaiah 55:11 tells us that God's Word is powerful and effective. We don't need to soften certain passages or be afraid of presenting it unmediated.

• Preach for faithfulness to the message, rather than transformation of your hearers. Every pastor and Bible teacher hopes that people will be changed and be more like Christ because of his or her work. So who wouldn't laud the idea of making transformation the goal of our preaching and teaching? Remember, God has asked us to partner with Him, but He still leads the dance. He is the one, through His powerful and effective Word and the illumination of the Holy Spirit, who changes lives. Making faithfulness to the message our goal puts the burden on God and removes the temptation for us as messengers to over-innovate with "new measures" that take the focus off of God and His revealed truth.

One example: A few years back I preached a message on John 3:1-21. I spent the vast majority of the time explaining the exegetical details of the text rather than applying them. The main imagery of being in light or darkness and how belief informs that status was the point of the sermon. After explanation of all the details of the inspired author, the question virtually asks itself, "Are you in light or darkness?" I felt this was the author's unspoken point of the narrative, so I pressed the question and explained clearly what belief entailed but did not belabor the point. Several months later during one of our baptisms, one woman shared that it was during that message that she came to believe in Christ. There was no invitation or prayer. She simply came to believe as I did my best to bring out the inspired author's meaning.

• Adopt a more invested strategy for evangelism instead of tracts, door-to-door encounters, or similar approaches. If our lives embody the Gospel, there is no clearer way to let the Gospel speak than to invite non-Christians into our lives. Train your congregation to build long-term relationships with those who don't follow Christ. These are not project relationships, but simply an effort to help the congregation "live" outside of the church. Praying for opportunities to share the Gospel is obviously a high priority, but if none present themselves, that is okay. And after those conversations, maintain and continue to nurture the relationship. This will necessarily take away any gimmicks or exaggerations ("Jesus will make all of life great!") we might be tempted to employ and will allow for a fuller, truer picture of the Gospel to be communicated over time.

One example: Matt W. recently had a young lady join his college group who did not identify herself with Christ. But she came regularly, heard all their conversations, and observed their lives. She even traveled to Alaska with the group in Matt's old RV! Somewhere along the way she identified herself as a follower of Christ. Today she knows Christ and knows the Gospel. She observed and learned the fuller version over a more protracted period of time. In this case, it was as much caught as it was taught.

• Help people count the cost. We know that we are inviting people to what is best for them, even if it might bring inconvenience or much worse. Proclaiming the Gospel to all as Christ revealed it is more faithful to the message. Being honest and up front with potential converts about what Christ demands of those who follow Him is a service and kindness to people. It also helps prepare people for success in following Christ. Finally, it reinforces that God is at the center of the story by avoiding the misconception that the Gospel is primarily a personal benefit.

• Proclaim the Gospel in the context of a biblical worldview. The context of all Scripture can help take the emphasis off of us and put the focus back on God's unfolding drama of redemption. Putting the story of the crucifixion and resurrection in the context of Genesis 1 to Revelation 22 focuses the attention on God's faithfulness and glory throughout the ages.

One example: When given the opportunity in our services and in personal encounters, I almost always try to explain Christ's position as Lord of creation and crucified Savior in terms of the Fall (where we've come from) and Christ's return (where our future is). In today's culture it's not uncommon to have the idea of sin challenged, but virtually everyone knows intuitively that something about life is broken.

• Keep the Gospel above the cultural fray. The Gospel is the message of God's mercy and justice coming together in the person of Jesus. It has been the only way that people "must be saved" (Acts 4:12) for almost two thousand years. It is the revealed truth of God, and carries the message of the crucifixion and resurrection of the Son of God. We should communicate that sacred message in manners that signify its dignity and transcendence. Handle that message in a way that sets it apart from many of our lesser passions, such as our favorite football team, favorite politician, or favorite beer. Let the Gospel speak, and keep it in the sacred category that it belongs in. Keeping it sacred helps us keep in mind that our God transcends our petty concerns.

• Don't over-innovate. Creativity in sharing the message of the Gospel is obviously good. But at times we have tried too hard, and our creativity gets in the way and steals the show. The Gospel is based on a set of rational propositions that must be understood to be responded to appropriately. Drama, images, or music can help the message, but can also drown it out. Try letting the Gospel speak for itself and see what God might do.

Chapter 6
Interpret Actively and Faithfully
By Matt Whitman

Perhaps the simplest remedy to the concerns raised in the first part of this book is for us simply to be consistent in what we say and do. Once we've identified what we ought to do, the trick is figuring out how we as flawed people dependent on God's grace lead with consistency in a fallen world. In this short chapter, I'll suggest that one proposal that can help us avoid the pitfalls presented by the four cultural realities discussed in chapters one through four is to become an agent of interpretation. When we actively interpret both the obvious and subtle meanings of what the world is doing and what we are doing in ministry, we are better equipped to lead for the purposes of God's glory, and more likely to demonstrate actions consistent with our words and beliefs.

I've never heard anyone, let alone someone involved in ministry, say, "I'm not a big fan of consistency. I don't mind if my beliefs and actions line up or not." Every reasonable person wants to be consistent, and every reasonable person strives for it. It's painful when a friend (or maybe worse, an enemy) points out that what we're saying and what we're doing in ministry aren't in full agreement. I realize that the first part of this book may have been agitating for many readers (as it is for me) because we're charging inconsistency. Specifically, we're suggesting that, even though most ministers and lay leaders would agree that God is the central character of the church and the entire redemptive story of creation, we sometimes inadvertently say and do things that subtly run counter to that theological assumption.

Passages like Proverbs 19:1 and Matthew 5:33-36 (let your "Yes" be "Yes" and your "No" be "No") emphasize the importance of personal consistency, whereas consistency as a natural expression of obedience and faith is stressed in Hebrews 12:1-2. Aside from the fact that consistency demonstrates simple honesty, words and actions that are in keeping with our stated biblical values strengthen our witness and our ministry.

Consistency reinforces what we claim to believe. Inconsistency quietly undermines our message and purpose. Since American cultural assumptions can make consistency difficult, we ought to scrutinize all aspects of our ministry and Christian culture very closely to be as sure as possible that what we say and do aligns with the Gospel and glorifies God. While we often succeed in filtering out content-oriented cultural evils, we are more likely to unwittingly adopt cultural assumptions and habits that seem harmless and normal at a glance, but that undercut our message and purpose on closer inspection. If our inconsistencies are most likely to happen when we don't carefully consider the meanings of the things we say and do, then intentional interpretation of what things mean and what we're communicating is a practice that can help us ensure that we convey things that are closely in keeping with the purpose of the church. We can be intentional by choosing to act as interpreters of words, actions, and cultural texts. Most pastors and lay leaders have put much effort into interpreting the Bible. I'm suggesting that we also apply those interpretive practices to the culture in which we live in order to help ensure maximum consistency.

In a moment, we'll briefly consider how this very simple constructive proposal addresses concerns raised in chapters one through four, but first, I need to define four key concepts discussed in this section.

Unspokens

Some things are communicated overtly and directly using words; others are communicated in less obvious ways. We all know that body language, facial expressions, and tone of voice can carry as much or more meaning than the spoken words that go along with them. But unspokens are much more than just how we say things conversationally; everything (living, inanimate, or abstract) communicates something. We easily intuit that a room filled with plush couches in a circle with candles and dim lighting communicates a different meaning than a gymnasium full of bleachers. People notice unspokens. They speak loudly and clearly, often even more so than our words do. We communicate directly with what we say and write, and we also communicate indirectly (and sometimes without any awareness or planning) through the swirling mass of cultural texts and abstract subtleties that we present deliberately or accidentally.

I often say that "stuff means stuff." I'm convinced that everything means something. Slang words, hairstyles, body language, logos, shapes, designs, brand names, different cuts of pants, and even each digit on the human hand has its own meaning or meanings. Because all things come with embedded meanings, all things are also subject not just to study scientifically (questioning what something is made of, how it responds to stimuli, etc.), but to interpretation (What does this mean?). Of course meanings will vary from culture to culture, so this can be an imprecise science. But even though the study of meanings has many variables, that doesn't mean that we can't "know" what things mean. We all "know" it isn't a compliment when another driver flips us off.

Christians (and especially Christian leaders) need to consider carefully the multitude of messages conveyed by any cultural text employed in a church setting. Please note that I'm not calling for the rejection of culture in church; that would be impossible since church itself is a culture and creates culture. I'm not advocating rigid legalism or a habit of constant critical negativity; God can be glorified in a multitude of styles and settings. What I am suggesting is that we should do our best to ensure that our unspoken messages are in keeping with what we claim to be about. Ultimately, what we say overtly and what we say implicitly ought to be unified in their purpose of exalting God. Because "stuff means stuff," active interpretation sets us up for success in our Christian endeavors.

Cultural Texts

Throughout this section I'll be using the expression cultural text, which is a catch-all expression used to describe anything produced by human culture. By this definition a cultural text could be anything: a car, fingernail polish, a fast-food product, or a flirtatious look. It's my contention that intentional consistency requires us to consider the layers of meanings assigned to and associated with a variety of cultural texts. All cultural texts have meaning. Some cultural texts are very subtle in their meaning, but other texts like painting, film, music, and literature by nature invite interpretation.

Active Interpretation

By this I mean the practice of thoughtfully and deliberately considering the meaning of cultural texts and Christian messages. Active interpretation is a habit; even something of a lifestyle. It is a practice that keeps the interpreter conscious of meanings and messages on the overt, but more importantly, on the less-than-overt levels. Further, this practice is in keeping with the call of 1 Thessalonians 5:21-22 to test everything, hold on to the good, and avoid every kind of evil.

How This Proposal Addresses Those Concerns Raised in Earlier Chapters

The Marketplace

Christian leaders who practice active interpretation are always on the lookout for places where we might misappropriate maxims from the marketplace in our churches and our individual relationships with God. Evaluating ideas for consistency will prevent marketplace truths, which revolve around the satisfaction of the individual, from determining the values of the church by neglectful default. In their place, biblical values focused on the glorification of God can be articulated directly and reinforced through unspoken messages.

Democracy

In a democratic system, we are called to determine the will of the people. However, when we make decisions in church, our task is to determine the will of God and abide by it. Being intentionally consistent means that we lead with that truth in mind, and say and do things overtly and in unspoken ways that only reaffirm Christ's headship over His church. This will require leaders to consider the meanings and implications of the systems we adopt to govern and manage our churches. These systems, like all things, are loaded with meaning.

Technology

As exemplified in chapter one, specific technologies and the idea of technological progress in general are loaded with meaning. Practicing active interpretation means that we are able to recognize that adopting certain technologies may send messages that are in unnecessary tension with the Gospel and the glorification of God. Say a church distributed to its congregation dual beer-can drinking helmets and gave instructions for believers to suck the communion wine into their mouths through the two straws that come with them. We would balk because the dual beer-can drinking helmet technology has different connotations than the much simpler communion cup. Both are technologies (though not complex), but they don't convey the same meanings. Of course, this is an absurd example, but the point is to prompt us to question what meanings are unintentionally conveyed by things like complex lighting, subwoofers, projection screens, smoke machines, or even a simple microphone. They all mean "stuff." Being consistent requires us to consider the totality of what we are communicating instead of just asking "What works?" We have to engage in the task of interpreting technological cultural texts if we are to bring them into harmony with our purposes.

Technology also comes with promises. It promises to meet our needs, but the Gospel contains the claim that God ultimately meets our needs. Might indiscriminately using technology to promote the Gospel compromise the message that God is ultimately our provider? Technology promises to ensure our comfort, but Christ calls us to take up our cross and follow Him (not very comfortable). If we endorse and employ technology at every turn for the purposes of convenience and comfort, might we be putting up an obstacle to obedience for ourselves and others? Active interpretation may not solve all of these tensions, but it helps us to ask questions about the meaning of things. This in turn helps us to make sure that we don't inadvertently permit our technology to communicate a rival Gospel, but instead that God remains at the center of our message and practice.

Entertainment

As with technology, seeking consistency requires that we become Christian interpreters of entertainment and other cultural texts. Christians in third-millennium America swim in waters filled with every kind of amusement and diversion. In addition to the natural pitfalls that can accompany diversion in general, there is also the concern of the values conveyed by our entertainment. How often do the media we consume directly contradict the values we claim to adhere to? This is precisely why we need to practice active interpretation — without it, we end up celebrating the exact opposite of what we truly affirm. Leaders need to be active and careful interpreters when aspects of the entertainment industry or mentality inevitably cross paths with the church in order to make sure their messages are yielded to the purpose of God's glory. The entertainment mentality is also defused when Christian leaders teach those in their care to interpret cultural texts with the exaltation of God in mind.

Constructive Practices

It's difficult to say what church, Christian faith, and Christian leadership might look like if we engaged in active interpretation for the purposes of greater consistency as it pertains to the ways in which the four cultural realities discussed in this book affect the church in third-millennium America. With that in mind, the following is a list of modest suggestions for ways we might employ active interpretation for the purposes of sharpening our message and practice. I believe these practices set us up to say what we mean to say at the spoken and unspoken levels and help us avoid pitfalls that confuse our message. Clearly, this list is by no means comprehensive, but my hope is that it might be a good starting point.

I've had the opportunity to implement (albeit imperfectly) this constructive proposal in various local church ministry settings over the last ten years. As I go through this list of how this proposal might look when put into specific action, I'll quickly mention a few relevant ministry experiences I've had.

• Disclose. Put your cards on the table. Tell people what you're doing, why you're doing it, and what results you're hoping for. When we are trying to achieve an objective indirectly or subversively, we are more likely to say and do things that aren't precisely in keeping with the point. When we're transparent with our goals, motives, and methodology, our rationale is always right out in front and there is less room for confusion or mixed messages. Disclosure requires that we take the relevant results of our active interpretation and make them known to the people we're ministering to.

In our college and youth ministries, I've made a habit of offering disclosure statements when leading in worship. I might say something like this before we sing: "We're about to participate in worship through group singing. I've chosen songs that are reflective of what we believe biblically and we're going to try to present the music with artistic excellence. Anytime we do this we're mingling cognitive truths about God with an expressive artistic response; in other words, we're doing something that might allow us to offer worship to God through the interplay of the substance of what we sing and the emotional response to those truths. However, you need to know that as leaders we aren't looking for a certain response, mood, or energy from you; we don't need that for this time to be successful. We will not work you for any reaction, because that doesn't fulfill the purpose of worship. Our time of worship here is successful if God is worshiped and glorified." The point isn't exactly how I phrase such a statement (surely it's clumsier than that when it's live); the point is that I've communicated what's happening, how the leadership conceives of it, what is or isn't expected, and how we define success.

I've attended evangelistic meetings or weeks of Bible camp where speakers have started out their first talk by saying, "Right from the beginning, I want you to know that my goal is to see any of you who aren't believers right now make a commitment to Jesus by the end of the week." I may or may not take exception to what happened after that, but I appreciate their willingness to disclose. They realized that it's better to be transparent than to be sneaky. In doing so, they communicated to their audience on multiple levels that they believe in the message, that they respect those in attendance enough to tell them what they're trying to accomplish, and that salvation is the work of God and not a result of their methods.

Disclosure reduces the likelihood of spiritual manipulation and clarifies purposes and expectations. It is a practice that also gives leaders the opportunity better to maintain consistency in the spoken and unspoken messages of the church.

• Model and provide opportunities to interpret cultural texts. Formally or informally engage in book or film discussion groups. When doing so, evaluate meaning as well as raw content and consider aspects of the cultural text that are consistent and inconsistent with biblical values. This will help to nurture a church full of people better equipped to actively interpret for the purposes of consistency.

We've done this in our local church college ministry in two ways. First, we've held book and film discussion groups in which we focus on interpreting the meanings of the text as Christians. Second, we use the informal time at the beginning of many meetings to ask what movies attendees have taken in recently. Then instead of asking whether or not they "liked it," we consider what the film, and film in general, means and what about it might be redeeming or problematic.

• Actively examine the merits of cultural products from the Christian subculture. Seek out the highest quality Christian art (music, visual art, film, etc.) that best expresses or exists within biblical truth. Enjoy it and possibly even incorporate it thoughtfully while avoiding Christian cultural texts that elevate the individual. Be sure to include the best Christian art from the past.

• Consider carefully the language of personal revelation. Try to say things that are consistent with your doctrinal position on prophecy, revelation, and the work of the Holy Spirit. Be precise; if you mean to say that God spoke personally and directly to you, then use that language. If you mean instead to say that God seems to be prompting your heart toward an action, then use that language. Interpreting the meanings of such language improves clarity and can help to bring questions of personal leading into line with the purpose of glorifying God. Imprecise language fosters confusion. Clarity fosters edification and consistency.

• Embrace and promote deliberate language instead of vague sentimental language. At several funeral services I've heard believers preach that the deceased was "in heaven just looking down on us and smiling right now." Additionally, I've often heard well-intentioned Christian art wander into nice-sounding platitudes that are effective in greeting cards, but that fail to accurately represent orthodoxy. Evaluate what such language means. If it conveys truth it may have merit, but if it muddies the waters or effectively teaches falsehood, then the interpreting minister can find ways to lovingly recraft or redirect the sentimental language. Practice talking about God both anecdotally and formally in ways that are in keeping with biblical truth.

• Exercise restraint in the adoption of technology. Since the very use of technology communicates messages, it may be good to ditch your gadgets from time to time, and, in doing so, remove a competing message. It may be helpful to do worship services frequently with no electronic assistance. We've done this with our youth group to varying degrees. Some of the most focused, meaningful times of singing have been entirely instrument- and technology-free, and almost all of our most life-changing and group-changing moments have been almost entirely technology-free. People still have the capacity and, I believe, the desire to worship and interact with God without technology as a mediator.

• Audit your worship service. Sit down with leaders committed to intentional consistency and interpret your worship service. See what things communicate the centrality of God on the spoken and unspoken levels. Keep them or enhance them. See what things might glorify the individual on spoken and unspoken levels. Get rid of them or change them.

• Audit your facilities. There may be little you can do to change most details of your ministry facilities; however, the exercise is still valuable and may reveal important realities. As in the previous point, gather leaders and interpret your facility. Consider ways that it might better align with the purpose of the church.

• Audit your church ministries. Do the same things as the last two points, but this time interpret the meaning of your ministry programs. Seek to bring them into consistency on the spoken and unspoken levels with what you say church is supposed to be about.

• Take sin seriously. If you believe that it is a serious problem, put practices in place to address it and then stick to them. The point isn't to carry out an inquisition against congregants; the point is to bring the spoken and unspoken messages of how sin is handled into consistency with the rest of the message.

• Remind church members that the priority in meetings is to determine God's will. To emphasize this point further, consider requiring church members to agree to have been engaged in Bible reading daily for a certain period of days, weeks, or months prior to speaking or voting at a meeting. This reinforces the message that Christ is the Head of the Church.

• Lead by example in how you treat marginalized people. We can't escape how much Jesus talked about the poor and the outcasts. In some way, we need to model a Christ-like concern for them as a matter of consistency and as a matter of obedience. An interpreting Christian community will note that the messages of our words and our actions line up when we do this, and it will also speak volumes to the non-Christian world who watch what Christians are about.

• Ask around. Culture changes quickly; if you aren't sure of how to interpret something, ask someone spiritually mature who might have a better idea. This is a good idea even if you think you understand something. Such investigation offers insight as to how others (individuals and society) are interpreting a given cultural text.

Chapter 7

Embrace Substance

By Mark Coddington

Like consistency, substance is something that, on its face at least, is difficult to argue against. Entire libraries can be filled with books and study guides telling Christians how they can go deeper in their faith or understand the Word of God in a more substantive way. Likewise, virtually every pastor believes he is offering depth and substance in his preaching — at least as much as he believes his listeners can handle.

We are not condemning those efforts as misguided, nor are we arguing that they cannot produce fruit. Instead, we applaud those contributions — to the extent that they legitimately point the believer toward a more substantive understanding of God's character and the world He has created — and we offer a robust challenge to do more. As pure-hearted as many of those offerings have been, they have amounted to only a makeshift barrier against the incoming tide of vapidity and anti-intellectualism within modern American culture. That current needs something much stronger from the church to break its flow.

What we are advocating is a dramatic shift in priorities, a wholehearted embrace of the consequential and the substantive. The penetrating and profound can still be found within our culture. Every once in a while, it bubbles up to the surface in the form of a book or movie that rises to popularity, or a tragic event that pierces and exposes our shallow, everyday concerns. But most of the time, it stays hidden, buried beneath the frothy fluff of whatever's new, whatever's now. We charge Christians and their churches to become attuned to that undercurrent and to encourage others to plumb its depths so that they might find the richness that lies below.

Though at times living with an eternal perspective requires paying attention to the immediate, God is continually calling His people throughout His Word toward a deeper understanding of reality that eschews the trivial and the seemingly pressing. Perhaps the Apostle Paul articulates this charge most explicitly when he calls the Corinthians to fix their eyes "not on what is seen, but on what is unseen" (2 Cor. 4:18). His rationale is particularly telling: "For what is seen is temporary, but what is unseen is eternal." The easiest way to lose touch with what is ultimately real, Paul says, is to focus on what seems most real — whatever is right in front of us, is easiest to access and digest, clamors for our attention. It is when we make an effort to go beyond that, to find the subtle, the difficult-to-grasp, the unlooked-for, the unseen, that we find what is truly eternal.

The book of Ecclesiastes has a remarkably similar message, though from a far different vantage point. The Teacher has tried everything — pleasure, fame, work, even wisdom for its own sake — and the missing piece of his existential puzzle is meaning. He has lived, by almost any worldly measure, a full life, but one completely without substance. The prescription for readers to avoid the same fate is to "fear God and keep His commandments" (Eccl. 12:13). And the greatest commandment, Jesus says later, is to love the Lord — an unseen, ineffable, mysterious, infinitely deep God — with all our heart, soul, mind, and strength (Mark 12:10).

The Bible presents growth for the Christian not as an optional, if-you-feel-like-it add-on, but as an indispensable part of the Christian life (1 Pet. 2:2, 2 Pet. 3:18). That growth requires substance, advancement from the elementary truths of the faith to its deeper truths.

To Paul, this comes through a refusal to be conformed to concerns of the world and a continual transformation that comes through the renewing of the mind (Rom. 12:2). The author of Hebrews lays out a similar course when he admonishes his audience for needing to be re-taught the basics of righteousness when, he says, "by this time you ought to be teachers" (Heb. 5:12). According to the author, the idea of Christian growth is a natural progression from taking in "milk" (simple, basic principles) to "solid food" (deeper, richer principles and teachings). Christians weren't meant to stay in the first stage, though many seem content to.

Of course, substance can exist outside of the explicitly Christian. Our search for substance cannot exclude these sources. Indeed, as the well-worn maxim puts it, "all truth is God's truth," and God is just as capable of revealing Himself through the writings of a hardened atheist like Hemingway as any of the books on the shelf of our local Christian bookstore. Still, as the Teacher in Ecclesiastes makes clear, a life spent pursuing the ponderous, too, is meaningless when it is done for its own sake. We are not calling for substance in and of itself, as if a month spent reading Foucault and Dostoevsky were all American evangelicals needed to cure their spiritual ailments. But we are urging Christians to embrace it with an understanding that God is found not only in the noise and chaos of entertainment, pop culture, technology, or the marketplace, but even more so in the quietness of an epiphany, in the subtlety of the unseen, in the mystery of the profound.

How This Proposal Addresses Those Concerns Raised in Earlier Chapters

It's not hard to see how this suggestion addresses the concerns we've brought up in this book's previous chapters. Substance often gets suppressed in a marketplace society that appeals to the lowest common denominator. The most popular or "best-selling" ideas are the ones that the majority of people find personally appealing and least disruptive to adopt, though they may have little eternal value or, as is often the case, run counter to biblical principles. Meanwhile, the truly meaningful ideas have far less mass appeal while holding far greater richness and joy for those who live by them. If the church's barometer for ideas and practices becomes the degree to which they line up with carefully thought-out biblical principles rather than their perceived success or marketability, we might be a little less popular but a lot more grounded in the glorification of God.

This new focus is a welcome remedy for a democratic society that tends to choose ideas or leaders by treating the substance of all ideas as equal and voting for the more popular one, or the one with the charismatic spokesperson or the one that just feels right to us. By contrast, the church must wrestle through issues, judging the soundness of ideas and behaviors through a robust understanding of the full context of Scripture. This cannot be done effectively without a worldview that appreciates the importance of serious instruction in biblical themes and the application of Christian principles. Our source of authority is not our own collective power, but Scripture, making an earnest effort to delve into its complex themes essential to our spiritual prosperity.

It's also an ideal response to a world in which technology has enabled us to do just about anything with the push of a few buttons. Where technology's ease and convenience often diminishes knowledge and our connection with each other and the natural world, a lifestyle that seeks the consequential will strengthen our ties with our fellow humans, help us understand their struggles and joys more deeply, and keep us more in touch with the world God has created. It's tough to talk theology through text messaging — or anything else of substance, for that matter. But a conscious emphasis on the things that matter will help break down those technological barriers we've built to shield ourselves from the reality of both our helplessness before an almighty God and the all-important salvation He has provided.

Of the cultural realities we've discussed, the one this proposal best combats is our culture's elevation of entertainment through the prevalence of visual media. The Gospel, by its very nature, calls for our thoughtful interaction with weighty, eternal ideas. It urges us to contemplate the unseen, to ponder our eternal destination, to recognize our own smallness before an infinite God. If it does not cause us to confront these concepts, then it is not the Gospel, but our own easy distortion of it. And as Christians, it does our souls good to be pulled out of the day-to-day scramble for our attention and to be reminded of these deeper realities that were so central in drawing us to Christ in the first place. Anything that can further attune us to these realities should be welcomed into the Christian life with open arms. As we mentioned earlier, God has preserved the written Word for us to encounter Jesus, the living Word. Spending time on that which requires thought trains Christians to be better thinkers and more active readers when they encounter Christ through the Word. A life of substance also challenges us to keep from adopting the passive attitude that comes with an entertainment-driven culture. It requires believers to take an active and engaged stance as we work through and live out our faith. It forces us to stretch ourselves and, when embraced by a Christian community, helps us to "spur one another on toward love and good deeds" (Heb. 10:24).

Constructive Practices

So what do we mean when we talk about embracing substance? There's no one-size-fits-all definition, but generally we mean making an effort to consume and create art, media, entertainment, and biblical teaching that challenges us, pushes us to evaluate our assumptions about life and faith, and deepens our understanding of what it means to live as Christians. These substantive experiences may not overtly ask these questions or make these points — though they certainly do at times —

but they will at least help attune us to these issues and help keep our mental engine in gear so that matters of eternal significance are never far from our minds.

Here are some practical proposals for finding this balance and helping others find it, too. Feel free to chew on them a bit, find out which ones might work for you, and try out a few of your own, too.

• It all starts on an individual level. Thanks to the convenience of the internet, we have more access to substantive writings, movies, music, and teachings than any culture in history. But it doesn't jump to the forefront, so we have to make an effort to find it. Ask friends you respect what works have challenged and stretched them. Check out thoughtful Christian reviews like Books & Culture. Seek out more comprehensive examinations of current events than the shouting heads on cable television or the brief roundup in your daily newspaper.

• Consider more carefully not just the content (such as words or images that we might find offensive), but the underlying ideas and messages of your cultural consumption. As we pointed out in an earlier chapter, the content of our media often becomes a red herring to distract from those more subtle, but more significant, ideas they communicate to us. Content is certainly important, but an equal concern should be the deeper substance of the media we consume.

• Cultivate a culture of depth, conversation, and thought throughout your church. An easy starting point is to consistently offer opportunities to engage quality media, books, and ideas. Try innovative approaches to new or potentially complex material in church. My church offers opportunities for in-depth study on a variety of subjects, such as one current book group studying the origins of pagan religions. The forums give participants a chance to interact with faith-related ideas in a setting that encourages inquisitive questions and robust discussion.

• Encourage solid biblical teaching in your church. Most preachers tie their preaching to the Bible in some way, but many simply use it as a launching pad for personal reflections that may or may not be biblical, rather than as the cornerstone and anchor for instruction. Substantive biblical preaching does far more than refer to Scripture; it engages it in a robust way that's continually digging for deeper understanding, in addition to using it to affirm or justify what is already believed.

• Engage church history. The history of the faith is home to a wealth of experiences, saints, and theological challenges that can enrich, encourage, and stretch the believer. Many evangelicals, though, are largely blind to church history beyond the past few decades. Churches can help open up this fount of spiritual substance by offering classes, book studies, or even sermon anecdotes that tie church history to contemporary issues of faith.

My church has held several classes for interested congregants on church history that include engagement with key academic texts and field trips to connect our discussions with the world outside our church's walls. For example, I was part of one class on early American church history in which each participant read a book on one aspect of the subject, then made a presentation to the class and wrote a review. The reviews were then assembled and published as a resource for others in the church, and the group took a trip to New England following the class to see many of the places they'd read about. Twenty-three people participated over the course of the semester, with 15 submitting reviews. This is a particularly academic application, but churches can just as easily work to incorporate the church's historical practices, as well.

• Pull back the curtain on seminary-level thought and information in church teaching. By doing this, we help congregants add needed context and depth to their understanding of Scripture. We may often assume that lay people can't handle this level of biblical and theological instruction, but they often can if it's explained clearly and connected to ideas with which they are already familiar. Many of them, in fact, crave it but don't have time or opportunity to pursue it on their own. This proposal is an attempt to disabuse people of the notion that seminary-level knowledge is only for spiritual and intellectual elites; rather, it should be available for anyone with the desire to learn.

• Encourage churchgoers to accept the challenge of not being able to understand everything said in church. This is a corollary to our prior suggestion: If we are opening our churches to seminary-level information, many churchgoers will not understand all of it, and some will not understand much at all. The natural response by churchgoers is to complain or check out, and churches often respond to that by simplifying the material presented. But congregants should be encouraged to realize that if they have difficulty understanding what is taught, it is not necessarily the teacher's fault, but an encouraging sign that they are being challenged to grow. This is a difficult but necessary attitude shift if a Christian community is to embrace substance as a body. This principle could work especially well when accompanied by a strong support system that ensures that other avenues are available within the church for congregants to understand complex concepts

• Feel the freedom to work through issues slowly, considering all their implications and allowing for rich discussion and contemplation. This applies to issues of church direction from the church board as well as to Sunday school studies, and everything in between. Correspondingly, this requires nurturing the attention span of churchgoers as well. Help your congregation understand that your primary concern as a church, and as Christians, is not quantity, but quality.

• Cultivate opportunities to interact with the ideas you present. Allow your church's ministries to go beyond a passive, purely receptive experience. Point interested listeners to deeper resources on teaching subjects. Encourage discussion of sermons, teaching, and ministries through groups, meetings, or panels, particularly when there might be disagreement. Always make more available, and encourage churchgoers to take advantage of the opportunity.

• Carefully examine what your church is communicating through its use of and references to media and technology. If the medium is the message and the form of a message can convey as much meaning as its content, then we ought to examine how our messages in church are being presented. Take a close look at what media you're using in your worship services, sermons, and ministries and what they're communicating: Do they encourage thought and depth, or are accessibility and entertainment unduly elevated?

• Allow worship practices that resonate with the full range of human emotion and experience. There is a place for happiness in worship services. But there is also a place for pain, sorrow, brokenness, ambiguity, and duty. Find and embrace worship music, drama, testimonies, and other practices that create room for those experiences, thus connecting Christianity to the whole of the human experience, rather than just the most pleasant parts of it.

• Build in time to develop substantive relationships. This applies on both an individual and church-wide level. Set aside time for people that is simple, interactive, and technology-free, and learn to relish the unadulterated company of others, and encourage this on a whole-church scale through small groups or church-wide events. Build time into church activities and ministries for people to relate to one another, whether organically or more intentionally. This might mean de-emphasizing the demands of a schedule, rather than emphasizing it so much that relational depth is thwarted. More than almost anything else, our interactions with others show what it means to be flawed yet faithful humans relating to a glorified and gracious God.

Chapter 8

Strive for Simplicity

By Matt Ostercamp

Our fourth constructive proposal is for churches to strive for simplicity. Simplicity here does not necessarily mean easy, nor does it mean "dumbed-down," as in simple-minded. Simplicity is not the opposite of substance rather it clears space for the substantial. Simple is straightforward and direct with minimal abstractions, distractions, and complications. Simplicity also acknowledges our limits and God's provision. It is easily content and can rejoice in all things.

The call to follow Christ is not an easy call, but it is a simple one. We are to follow Him, trusting in His power to save us, rather than in our own pious works. Jesus explicitly warns against praying like pagans who babble on, thinking they will be heard because of their many words (Matt. 6:7). Instead, He offers the Lord's Prayer, with its simple affirmations and requests as the model to His disciples. He is also critical of public displays meant to highlight our piety (Matt. 6:2, 16) and severely chastises the Pharisees for subverting the direct teaching of God with their religious traditions (Mark 7:9-13). We believe these passages challenge us to keep things simple. Adding the proverbial bells and whistles to our worship is likely to bring more attention to the worshiper than the one being worshiped. Further, we believe these passages warn against creating the expectation that only skilled professionals can practice religion. We don't need great rhetorical powers to address God, nor can we pay others to fulfill our duty to our parents (Mark 7:19-13). We affirm doing things ourselves, either as individuals or local congregations, as simpler than relying on professionals from outside of our context.

Simplicity also applies to how we spend our time. Isaiah wrote, "This is what the Sovereign Lord, the Holy One of Israel says, 'In repentance and rest is your salvation, in quietness and trust is your strength'" (Isa. 30:15). Rest and quietness remind us that salvation and strength are the Lord's to bestow. A quiet, simple space may prove more conducive for us to hear from the Lord.

Finally, Christ teaches us not to worry about what we wear or eat but to trust the Lord's provision (Matt. 6:25ff). We believe that as we simplify our ministries and lives it becomes easier to acknowledge and accept God's blessings. Peter reminds us that true beauty does not come from outward adornment (1 Pet. 3:3-4) and likewise, true joy is not something we can buy or manufacture. Instead, as we strive for simplicity we hope to affirm, like Paul, that everything is a loss compared to the surpassing greatness of knowing Christ Jesus (Phil. 2:8). Undeterred by life's complexity and distractions we want to be able to rejoice in the Lord always (Phil. 4:4).

How This Proposal Addresses Those Concerns Raised in Earlier Chapters

Simplicity helps to minimize the manipulation that often arises when importing practices from the marketplace. Keeping things simple underscores that the church is a supernatural body whose power comes from the living God. Striving to keep things simple, we seek to dispel the myth that constant activity, strong brands, and witty advertising will usher in the Kingdom. We also believe that simplicity will help us overcome the consumer mindset that is easy to bring to worship. By requiring our direct engagement and participation, simple worship moves us beyond being passive observers. It reminds us that all are called to worship as an offering to God and that this reality takes priority over our individual tastes and preferences. Rather than catering our programs and message to target audiences and niche demographics, we ought to strive for simple practices that are widely accessible and build unity within the body.

Our democratic culture encourages us to get involved with the political process. Usually this means identifying with a party or cause and working diligently for its success. This type of political participation almost always becomes complicated as we work to build coalitions and are forced to accept compromise. The call to simplicity is a call to try to minimize the political intrigue that goes on in our churches. We believe that worrying about advancing our cause in church is often analogous to worrying about what we will wear. Although we may be called to bear witness to the truth as we understand it, ultimately we can rest knowing that God cares deeply about His church, and His power, not our cleverness, will sustain it. Simplicity allows us to speak and listen directly with one another and to rest from ceaseless campaigning as we affirm, in faith, God's control over His church.

Most of us are continually interacting with technological devices that enhance our power. Cumulatively, these devices promise us that we can control and manipulate our world to ensure our happiness. Striving for simplicity helps to dispel the illusions that we need our technology in order to live well. Technology also encourages us to interact with the world abstractly as we manipulate machines that do the actual work. Simplicity brings into clarity our dependence upon God — the true source of everlasting joy. Technology, like the water in the well at Sychar, will soon leave us thirsty again and is a poor substitute for the living water that we receive from Christ.

Our entertainment culture promises us never-ending diversion to keep us distracted. Simplicity helps us carve out quiet places away from this racket to encounter God as He is. The entertainment paradigm also promotes passivity, teaching us to take in the show that others have produced. As we simplify, we encourage active participation in worship and service rather than leaving it to the experts. Finally, prioritizing simplicity helps counter the allure to add rhetorical flourishes to the Gospel message that ultimately distract us from receiving it.

Constructive Practices

The following is a list of practices that I believe are helpful in applying the proposal to strive for simplicity. You may already be engaging in many of these practices, and I hope this list affirms and encourages you. Other suggestions might prompt you to think of new ways to simplify your ministry even further.

• Explicitly teach the biblical value of simplicity.

• Seek to model simplicity in the mode of public instruction and in the content of that instruction. Avoid making things more complicated or abstract than they need to be, but instead present material in a direct, straightforward manner at a pace that allows the audience to follow along. On the surface, this may seem contradictory to the previous chapter, in which we called for the embrace of substance. However, while we are calling for an emphasis on depth, we also believe that depth is best communicated in a simple style that doesn't detract from the point or use busyness and gimmicks to give a false impression of substance.

• Occasionally minister with less technology than usual to break our dependence upon it. One possibility would be meeting outside surrounded by God's creation to remind us that we can meet God anywhere, not just in formally sacred space.

Strive for Simplicity

One of my favorite Sundays of the year is our annual baptismal service on the shore of Lake Michigan. We rejoice in the testimony of the new believers flanked by tall shade trees with the wide lake vista behind us. This setting is enhanced by passing bikers and the curious onlookers. Without the usual conveniences of a modern church, we sit on the grass and are reminded of the beauty of salvation.

• Meet people's basic needs as a form of simple service to our neighbors. This helps us directly obey the commands of Christ and reminds us all of our shared dependence upon God's blessings. Examples include:
- Preparing food and serving it to others, especially those who may be hungry or struggle to provide their own meals.
- Building or repairing homes to provide shelter to those who are homeless either through poverty or disaster.
- Collecting, mending, and cleaning used clothing to give away to our neighbors.

• Revitalize and respect traditions and common practices of your church as anchors of stability amid a world of change. Singing songs that everybody knows or other familiar worship practices can be tools to focus on God rather than be distracted by trying to grasp the unfamiliar. It also reinforces continuity over time, which is a simpler idea than the common belief that each generation must carve its own path.

• Collectively agree upon ways to practice the Sabbath and help each other practice regular rest in a world that celebrates constant activity.

• Teach and practice actual fasting as a way of simplifying life and making time to worship God.

PUTTING GOD IN HIS PLACE

• Similar to fasting, the Christian discipline of silence can be revived as a way to draw our minds to God and away from the constant noise of the world.

• Corporately, a local church may choose to "fast" for a set time from curriculum, programming, songs, and other aids to worship purchased from outsiders, choosing instead to highlight local gifts and focus on basic truths.

• Churches may also suspend ministry and meetings for a period of time to encourage people to slow down, rest, and reflect.

One way our church encouraged rest was by declaring a Sabbath week — a week where all church and small group activities were cancelled. All members of the congregation were encouraged to spend time alone with God during the week in place of the usual hustle and bustle of ministry.

• Intentionally set aside places without any media or marketing for personal or group use.

• Engage in simple corporate celebrations as a Christian community — celebrating what God has done for us. Unfortunately, many of our holy days (or holidays) have become complicated by commercialization and cultural expectations that have little to do with celebrating with our spiritual family. Therefore, local congregations may wish to establish their own holy days such as:

- Annual baptism Sunday
- Celebration of a key date in the history of the local church

- Celebrating either the beginning or end of the Sunday school year
- Revisiting feast days from the Christian past

• Encourage people to spend leisure time exploring God's creation as a simpler way to pass time than many of the entertainment options presented by our culture. Time spent in natural settings is also likely to occasion worship and awe in the creativity and provision of our God.

• Model short, direct prayers and/or use the Lord's Prayer or other common prayers either individually or corporately to simplify the process of prayer and remove the focus from the individual who is praying.

• Don't allow schedules to tyrannize meetings, but allow the content presented and needs of the members to dictate the pace. Be especially wary of adding material to a schedule just to fill out the time; instead, keep the schedule as simple as possible.

• Encourage the local body to create curriculum and ministries that meet local needs. Often local solutions will be more straightforward than importing a program from another context, and the local congregation will have more control over the results.

• Make ministry choices that create realistic long-term spiritual expectations. Simplicity avoids hype and the promises of easy solutions apart from regenerative work of the Holy Spirit.

• Strive to unify worship services around a clearly communicated theme. Rather than have the audience try to puzzle out how or if the different components of the service cohere, make sure the relationship is apparent. Simplifying worship by reducing the number of elements will often increase clarity.

Conclusion

Taken literally, the title of this book is absurd. God can't be put in His place. He is in His place. No one can dictate anything to God. He's always been at the center, He continues to be at the center, and it's the position He'll always occupy. If it appears to us that God isn't at the center, the problem is with our perspective not God. We need to address that problem, which, in part is caused by our reckless adoption of subtle cultural values that prompt us to place ourselves in the position of ultimate esteem. In truth, we need to put ourselves in our place. That way we can rightly see and be reminded that, despite our illusions, God has been in His place all along, and we need to reconcile our thought and action with that reality.

Each generation of the church has had its challenges. The exaltation of the individual is ours. We abide in a culture obsessed with the self, and that value is the single most contrary value to a right relationship with God. No outsider or rival planted those insidious values in our midst. Rather, we ourselves brought the "gifts" of third-millennium America within the walls of the church only to find there were malevolent forces lurking inside. The church must be aware of these forces and engage them with wisdom, discernment, courage, and the power of the Holy Spirit if we are to succeed in keeping God at the center.

We're a part of the battle, and a part of the problem. Whatever failings we've pointed out in the church are our failings as well. Still we have hope for the church and we remain committed to it, as He remains committed to us. Although we've identified urgent and dangerously subtle challenges to the church, we see the focal point of this book as the constructive proposals you've just read. Our challenge comes at us from all points of the cultural compass, and requires a multi-faceted response. Our proposals can only serve as a rough first step. Specific action depends on you.

In the face of forces that would exalt the individual, we reassert that the church exists for the glory of God. We must engage this from the perspective of John the Baptist who demonstrated the right understanding of His position in relation to God's when he said, "He must increase, but I must decrease."

Appendix
The Purpose of the Church
By Aron Utecht

Why Does the Church Exist?

    To answer the question, let me begin in an unlikely place, Genesis 1. As it is recorded for us, God is the originator of all things created, including humans. Yet humans have a special place in the created order. Before God pronounces His assessment of His own work, calling it very good, he completes the final piece of the puzzle. Humans, both man and woman singly and in their relationship together, bear the image of God. God places His own image upon His creatures. He is willing to link His own identity (though not, of course, His nature) with His creatures! Even more, He gives them a really great commission, "Go and rule over the rest of creation on my behalf, and fill the rest of the earth with the image that I have bestowed on you." It was God's first intention that His people, which before the Fall included all humans, should exist to reveal His nature and character among all the rest of creation. As humans went out into the earth to fill it, they took with them the divine image. In biblical parlance, we would say that the purpose of God's first people was to glorify Him.

    Very shortly after those events, though, Scripture records for us the events of the Fall. Adam and Eve, and all who follow in their line, are out of the fold. So God begins the process of redeeming a people for Himself who would bear His name (2 Sam. 7:23). As the narrative moves forward, we see that all the peoples of the earth are corrupt (Gen.

10-11), so God does not choose any of the nations but decides instead to create His own nation who will serve Him (Gen. 12). Beginning with Abram, God created the people of Israel. In time, they became a nation, with a culture that included religious observances, moral standards, and structures for governance and leadership, all for the purpose of revealing the holy character of God. Even as they lost their status as a nation, elaborate rules evolved as an attempt to fulfill their task of revealing God's character.

Some believe that the church has replaced the nation of Israel in God's plan, and others believe that the church is a new addition to the story. But all will agree that the New Testament church has now come to be included among God's people (Acts 15:14). In discerning why the church exists, then, we can take some important cues from Israel, God's covenant people from the Old Testament. Time after time, Scripture records that the result of God's miraculous deliverance for His people is Him receiving honor both from His people and the other inhabitants of the earth. In Numbers 14, where God considers destroying Israel to begin a new people with Moses, Moses' chief argument against such a course is that the Egyptians will perceive it as a failure on God's part.

Perhaps Isaiah 43 states most clearly that God bestowed His love on Israel for His purposes. He redeemed them out of sin and called them to be His people for His glory and His purposes. Even forgiveness of sin was primarily for God's sake. The benefits that the members of His community receive from that forgiveness are secondary to the primary purpose of being purified to be His witnesses (see especially Isa. 43:7-13, 25).

The same is true of the New Testament community of God's people: God is at the center of the story, after all, and not humans. The New Testament writers pick up this theme and repeat it often. Paul tells us that those called into relationship with Him are specifically called to reflect the character of Christ, who just happens to be the perfect image of God (Rom. 8:29, Col. 1:15). In Titus 2:14 he uses language very similar to David, stating simply that God has redeemed and purified a people for His purposes (2 Sam. 7:23). John records Jesus telling His disciples that those who follow Him are to bear fruit for the Father's glory (John 15:8). Peter also affirms that the New Testament community is a new type of spiritual "nation" without boundaries or ethnicities, meant to declare the works and character of God (1 Pet. 2:4, 9-10). Three times in Ephesians 1 Paul emphasizes the idea that the New Testament community has been called and blessed toward the end of glorifying God (Eph. 1:6, 12, 14).

In much the same vein as the Old Testament community of faith, the New Testament community has been assembled for the purpose of being a witness to the character, nature, and works of God. The New Testament church does not exist for itself, but for God's purposes, to be a witnessing community that goes out into the earth and truthfully "images" the true Creator. The church exists to glorify God.

This is affirmed in the various ways to describe the church. Each engages a different aspect of God's own creation, where He is to be made known. God, of course, is Spirit, and it is natural that to truly reflect His character well, the church must also be spiritual in nature. Yet Scripture also gives many instructions about the institutional nature of the church. God is a God of order, not chaos (1 Cor. 14:33), and many of the institutional principles given in Scripture are toward the end of reflecting that part of God's character. Through regeneration God purifies the church and unites us to Himself. But He has also provided mechanisms so that our functions and gatherings also reflect well on Him.

The same principle is at work in the local/universal distinction, too. In all its localized endeavors, whether witnessing, good works, or holy living, small or large bodies of Christians illustrate the character of God — His grace, mercy, love, justice, and holiness. But these local bodies are also part of a larger picture. Oftentimes various churches will band together (even across denominational or regional boundaries), to support mission or relief works. And using Genesis 1:26-28 as a continuing paradigm, the universal church completes a bigger picture throughout the world, indeed, filling the whole earth with His glory. This is what Paul is alluding to in Ephesians 1:23. Both the local and universal components of the church work to take God's glory into all the earth.

To refer to a church as a body is to highlight its corporate nature, yet each local body is obviously composed of individuals. God is equally concerned that the movement that bears the name of His Messiah and that the individuals who name Him reflect His character. The corporate church exists to glorify God. If an individual's actions are not congruent with that goal, then the Bible tells us they are to be removed until they are willing to change their behavior.

This raises the sticky question of who is in the church. Is it a place for believers only, or are unbelievers welcome, too? Church history illustrates the valiant attempts of some to purify the church and avoid mixed multitudes. These solutions raised their own problems, though, and Scripture seems to indicate that we ought to expect the uninitiated to join our services (1 Cor. 14:23-24).

After all, part of our mission is to convert and save those who are lost and send them back out as more image-bearers. This is vitally important to the big picture. In Genesis 1 it was the original commission of all humanity to take God's glory out into the world and fill it with the reflection of His good and perfect character. We should likewise be concerned to see people reconciled back to God and reacquainted with His general plan for their lives, so we want non-believers around and participating in the church. But it is not an involvement at all costs that we are looking for. If Jesus and Paul both affirm that those associating themselves with the church must strive for holiness or they're no longer welcome, then humans are not at the center of the story. God is the center of the story.

What are the purpose(s) of the church?

The overarching goal of Christ's church is to glorify God. We'll call that our strategy. Our tactics will involve many purposes that move us toward that goal. But the key is understanding each purpose in light of the larger Purpose, or they get out of balance and can mislead our practice. What we believe about the strategy will impact how we behave in our tactics. Here's just a few of the main purposes that move the church toward the larger goal.

Public worship — One primary purpose of local church bodies is to provide a place for individual believers to come together and worship God. In doing so, we proclaim His character and works (1 Pet. 2:9). Part of the worship service is also to provide an avenue for observing the sacraments. And while there are varying beliefs in how these specifically strengthen the believer, it is clear that they clearly speak of God's grace, mercy, and love in the Gospel, as well as His offer of new life in Christ (1 Cor. 11:26). Corporate gatherings also provide a place for preaching, which entails both the proclamation of the Gospel and instruction for the body (1 Cor. 14:26; 1 Tim. 4:13). All of these result in the glory of God. His perfect nature and wonderful work of salvation is proclaimed. His people acknowledged their humble dependence as His creatures, and individuals are instructed on how to better live and represent God in their sphere of influence.

Good works — Paul is clear in Ephesians 2:10 that God has given us the gift of salvation for a purpose — to go out and do good works on God's behalf. This is a tactic that ought to be engaged at both the corporate and individual levels. This is also a great way to have those who are unconverted join in the work of the church. Their efforts on God's behalf don't earn them any favor with God, but it is still pleasing to Him for His creatures to fulfill their ordained purpose. And it also has the benefit of giving non-believers a fuller picture of what it means to truly follow Christ. Whether it is helping the single moms in their neighborhood scoop a heavy snow or joining the universal church in worldwide relief efforts, Christians should be engaged in good works. Jesus perhaps summarized it best in John 15:8, "This is to my Father's glory, that you bear much fruit, showing yourselves to be my disciples."

Disciple-making — In Ephesians 4, Paul instructs that a major role of church leadership is to prepare and equip God's people for their mission. The goal is to build the body up, which results in unity and maturity for the church at the individual and corporate level. As people are grounded in doctrine and practice, they are not led astray into wrong ideas or behaviors. The mature believer can better reflect the character of God and better explain His gracious offer of salvation among a world that Jesus has promised will be hostile toward those who follow Him (John 16:1-4, 33; 2 Tim. 3:12).

An intentional effort on making disciples must be a tactic in the larger strategy of glorifying God. The church is to nurture obedience and holiness in individuals. The absence or neglect of that tactic could potentially bring us converts who wish to name Christ but continue to live in ways that don't honor Him.

Evangelism — As we've stated already, bringing others into the community of the redeemed is vital to God's plan to make Himself known through His people. And this should be done at both corporate and individual levels. Throughout church history, various movements have adopted a "come" approach, or a "go" approach, such as sending missionaries, door-to-door encounters, or having large events at churches or public places. All these approaches have their strengths and weaknesses, but each needs to be understood as a tactic in the larger strategy of taking God's image, an accurate representation of His character and works, out into the world. If we don't keep it in perspective with the broader goal of glorifying God, we will unintentionally reshape the message — which will be the subject of the next chapters.

Some Necessary Marks of Christ's Church

In third-millennium America, there is no shortage of organizations that describe themselves as a church. But for those of us who hold the Bible as the final arbiter, there are a few guidelines that we need to meet to allow ourselves to use the term for our own groups. Here are three important marks that any groups that identify themselves as followers of Christ ought to bear.

Faithful proclamation of the Bible — Any organization that claims to be a Christian church must proclaim the essential message of the Bible as contained in the Old and New Testaments. Of course, various churches will interpret this differently, and that isn't going away anytime soon. However, any church that misrepresents what the Bible says or neglects its message is stealing the term and the cultural capital that comes with it. An absence of an honest, earnest attempt at preaching the Bible's message and maintaining doctrinal purity excludes us from the category of "church" in the biblical sense.

Administration of the sacraments — Generally, Protestants will identify two sacraments that Jesus commanded His church to observe, communion (1 Cor. 11:23-26) and baptism (Matt. 28:18-20). While each church interprets the meanings and outcomes of these practices differently, all agree that they convey important theological truths. To neglect them is to deny two vital elements that set us apart as distinctively Christian. It is also blatant disobedience to the Lord's clear command for His followers.

Exercise of church discipline — We have already stated that the main goal of the church is to glorify God. It is only logical, then, that any who wish to identify themselves with Christ's church need to reflect the holy character of its Lord and Head. If after a patient and loving process of instruction and counseling, someone is still unwilling to strive for the standards in God's word, that person is to be removed from the fellowship (Matt. 18:15-20; 1 Cor. 5:1-5, 13). Local churches are to be local manifestations of God's character and nature. Those not willing to participate in that goal don't have the privilege of sullying the reputation of everyone else or the name of Christ. Of course, those willing to repent and submit to God's standards should be welcomed back to the community (2 Cor. 2:5-11).

This is far from exhaustive. We do not intend to be so here; others have done that far better than we could. We have not touched at all on the offices of the church, the relationship between the church, and the concept of the Kingdom. And we've said nothing about the relationship between the church and Israel or what part it plays in salvation's history. And we've said nothing about Christ as our Head, and His relationship to the church.

Two more things need to be briefly mentioned though before we continue. First, we cannot define the whole based on only one tactic. It is not uncommon at all to see a church with a heavy focus on either evangelism or discipleship. But understanding both as important tactics for achieving a broader strategy perhaps helps to relieve this tension. As church leaders strive to meet both goals, we need to keep in mind how to integrate the two so that resources of staff, time, and money are maximized, and the two aren't pitted against each other in the church.

It also needs to be stated that the New Testament is fairly silent on definitions for success. We see large numbers of converts in the narrative of Acts, yet we also see the small church of Philadelphia being commended for their faithfulness. In Colossians 1:28-29, Paul states his desire to present all under his care as mature in Christ. Perhaps we would do well to make these our twin standard as well: faithfulness to the message, and ability to develop those whom God gives to maturity.

The Purpose of the Church

The Church exists for the glory of God. The first four chapters of this book highlight how four cultural realities in third-millennium America work against Christians and compromise our success in glorifying God. By default we will exalt either ourselves or God. No one can serve two masters (Matt. 6:24).

Bibliography

Berkoff, Louis. Systematic Theology. Grand Rapids, Mich.: Eerdmans, 1938.

Bonhoeffer, Dietrich. The Cost of Discipleship. New York: Touchstone, 1995.

Borgmann, Albert. Power Failure: Christianity in the Culture of Technology. Grand Rapids, Mich.: Brazos, 2003.

Bucy, Erik P. and Melissa E. Grabe. "Taking Television Seriously: A Sound and Image Bite Analysis of Presidential Campaign Coverage, 1992-2004." Journal of Communication (December 2007): 652-675.

Carson, D.A. Christ and Culture Revisited. Grand Rapids, Mich.: Eerdmans, 2008.

Franklin, Benjamin. Autobiography. Ed. J.A. Leo Lemay and P.M. Zall. New York: W.W. Norton, 1986.

Gay, Craig M. The Way of the (Modern) World: Or, Why It's Tempting to Live As If God Doesn't Exist. Grand Rapids, Mich.: Eerdmans, 1998.

- Cash Values: Money and the Erosion of Meaning in Today's Society. Grand Rapids, Mich.: Eerdmans, 2004.

Hatch, Nathan O. The Democratization of American Christianity. New Haven, Conn.: Yale University Press, 1991.

Hipps, Shane. The Hidden Power of Electronic Culture: How Media Shapes Faith, the Gospel, and Church. El Cajon, Calif.: Youth Specialties, 2006.

Kingsolver, Barbara. Animal, Vegetable, Miracle: A Year of Food Life. New York: Harper, 2008.

"Information Behaviour of the Researcher of the Future." UCL. 11 January 2008. http://www.jisc.ac.uk/media/documents/programmes/reppres/gg_final_keynote_11012008.pdf.

McLuhan, Marshall and Quentin Fiore. The Medium Is the Massage: An Inventory of Effects. New York: Bantam, 1967.

Meyers, Kenneth A. All God's Children and Blue Suede Shoes: Christians and Popular Culture. Wheaton, Ill.: Crossway Books, 1989.

Niebuhr, H. Richard. Christ and Culture. New York: Harper & Row, 1951.

Noll, Mark A. America's God: From Jonathan Edwards to Abraham Lincoln. New York: Oxford University Press, 2002.

- The Scandal of the Evangelical Mind. Grand Rapids, Mich.: Eerdmans, 1995.

Pascal, Blaise. Pensees. London: Penguin, 1995.

Postman, Neil. Amusing Ourselves to Death: Public Discourse in the Age of Show Business. New York: Penguin, 1985.

Twitchell, James B. Shopping for God: How Christianity Went From in Your Heart to in Your Face. New York: Simon & Schuster, 2007.

Vanhoozer, Kevin J. Is There a Meaning In This Text? Grand Rapids, Mich.: Zondervan, 1998.

Wells, David F. No Place for Truth, or, Whatever Happened to Evangelical Theology? Grand Rapids, Mich.: Eerdmans, 1993.

Willard, Dallas. Renovation of the Heart: Putting on the Character of Christ. Colorado Springs, Colo.: Navpress, 2002.

- The Spirit of the Disciplines: Understanding How God Changes Lives. San Francisco: HarperSan-Francisco, 1991.

Citations

Page 41
Dietrich Bonhoeffer, The Cost of Discipleship, (Touchstone: New York), 1995, p. 89. – the First Touchstone (a Simon& Schuster Co) was 1995, the first English edition appears to have been 1959. The German translation was titled Nachfolge, 1937.

Page 47
D. A. Carson, Christ and Culture Revisited, (Eerdmans: Grand Rapids, MI), 2008, p. 127.

Page 50
Hipps, Shane, The Hidden Power of Electronic Culture: How Media Shapes Faith, the Gospel, and Church
(Grand Rapids, Mi.: Zondervan, 2005), 34.

Page 54
"Information Behaviour of the Researcher of the Future: A Ciber Briefing Paper" UCL, 11 January 2008,
http://www.jisc.ac.uk/media/documents/programmes/reppres/gg_final_key-note_11012008.pdf, p. 8.

Page 67 & 72
Postman, Neil. Amusing Ourselves to Death: Public Discourse in the Age of Show Business. New York: Penguin, 1985.

Page 67
Franklin, Benjamin. Autobiography (New York: W.W. Norton, 1986), 90.

Page 69
Bucy, Erik P., and Maria E. Grabe. "Taking Television Seriously: A Sound and Image Bite Analysis of Presidential Campaign Coverage, 1992-2004." Journal of Communication 57 (2007): 652-75.

Page 86
Pascal, Blaise. "Pensees." (NuVision Publications, LLC, 2007), 48.